THE DAY
MICHAEL COLLINS
WAS SHOT

A Paperback Original
First published 1989 by
Poolbeg Press Ltd.
Knocksedan House,
Swords, Co. Dublin, Ireland.

Text and Maps
© Meda Ryan 1989

ISBN 1 85371 041 5

Cover design by Pomphrey Associates
Maps drawn by Curly Cahalane
Typeset by Print-Forme,
62 Santry Close, Dublin 9.
Printed by The Guernsey Press Ltd.,
Vale, Guernsey, Channel Islands.

THE DAY
MICHAEL COLLINS
WAS SHOT

Meda Ryan

POOLBEG

When a good chess-player has lost a game and is fully persuaded that the fault was his own, he sets aside the blunders he may have committed during the progress of the game to examine what mistake he made at the beginning of which his adversary took advantage to compass his defeat. The game of war—a much more elaborate matter—is influenced by the conditions under which it is carried out, and far from being within the power of one single will, it is the outcome of the friction and shock of all the thousand wills and passions which are brought into play.

Leo Tolstoy, *War and Peace*

For Donal

Contents

Acknowledgements

As I look through my note book of names and addresses, I notice with sadness that many of those who willingly gave information are no longer with us. But without their generosity of spirit there would be no book.

A sincere word of gratitude is due to Jim Kearney and the late Neilus Flynn who sowed the initial seeds for my research, and were indirectly responsible for this book. I am deeply indebted to Domhnall Mac Giolla Phoil who went out of his way to locate people for me, and who, with his wife Mary, listened to my problems while I worked on the manuscript, and Eily Hales McCarthy and her husband Gus, who give me continuous encouragement.

Michael Collins (nephew of General Michael Collins) trusted me with his uncle's original notebooks. Ned Barrett also gave me affidavits which he had acquired over the years because of his personal interest in events relating to Michael Collins. I thank both sincerely.

Without the help of Dr. Leo Ahern, Dr. Gerard Ahern, Dr. Christy Kelly, Dr. Michael O'Riordan, Dr. Daniel Coghlan, the late Canon Joe Ahern and a representative of Dr. Cagney, this book would be incomplete.

I am indebted to the kindness of Raymond Smith and Jim Nicholl, both of Independent Newspapers, who unreservedly gave me information and guided me towards Jock McPeak's solicitor and the McPeak family. (The latest information available to me confirms that Jock McPeak spelled his name thus and not *McPeake* as many historians have believed.)

I am deeply grateful for the assistance and courtesy of the staff in the Archives Department of University College, Dublin, and to that Department for the use of material, also to the Mulcahy Trust for access to, and permission to quote from, the papers of Richard Mulcahy; to Kieran Burke and Tom McCarthy, Cork City Library, both of whom speedily responded to my queries; to Brid Frawley of the University of Limerick (N.I.H.E.) Library, who devoted some of her spare time to doing research for me; to Commandant Peter Young, Military Archivist, Cathal Brugha Barracks, Dublin who was so efficient in his responses to my queries, and to his assistant Sergeant Joe White; to the late Lieutenant Colonel Joseph Foley, Plunkett Barracks and Commandant David Collins and Lieutenant Tom Boyce, Cathal Brugha Barracks; to the staff at Collins's Barracks Dublin; to Brigadier General Kevin Nunan, Lieutenant Colonel Gerry Mulrooney, Captain O'Connor, Pat Lynch and the staff at the Curragh Military Barracks who explained the various types of arms and ammunition, who took me on a trip in the *Slieve na mBan* armoured car and who showed me around the premises; to Oliver Snoddy of the National Museum, Dublin who was extremely helpful with all my queries; to Noel Crowley and Mary Moroney, Ennis County Library; to the Library Staff at Mary Immaculate College, Limerick; to the Library Staff of *The Irish Independent, The Irish Times, The Irish Press* and *The Cork Examiner*; to the staff of *The Sunday Press, The Sunday Independent, The Clare Champion, The Limerick Leader* and *The Southern Star;* to the staff of Shanakiel Hospital, Cork, and to the Ordnance Survey Office.

The reponsive attitude of so many whom I interviewed over the years is deeply appreciated: Daniel Corcoran, Cormac McCarthaigh, Peg Cleary, Tommy Dineen, Dan Cahalane, Conchur O'Muineacháin, Tom Foley, Ned Galvin, Paddy Lynch, Con Murphy, Michael Murphy, Paddy Desmond, May Twomey, Jim Carmody, Dr. Paddy O'Sullivan, John L. O'Sullivan, Sean Byrne, Mary C. Duggan, Jerh. Galvin, Jack Mahony, Kathleen Donovan O'Driscoll, Kate O'Mahony, John Byrne, Hazel P. Smyth (B & I), Seamus O'Donovan, Brother John Nolan, Finbarr Murphy, Kathleen McCarthy, Agnes Kiely, John Joe

O'Sullivan, Rev. Canon Sean Piggott, Nuala Cuddy, Sean Collins-Powell, Michael Collins-Powell, Liam Collins and Cathal O'Shannon; also the late: Emmet Dalton, Ernest Blythe, Sean MacBride, Todd Andrews, Bill Powell, Timmy Sullivan, Madge Hales Murphy, Michael Brennan, Joe Dolan, Judge Fionan Lynch, Frank Aiken, Dan Bryan, Tom Kelleher, Pat Buttimer, Billy Barry, Jim Wolfe, Riobárd Lankford, Siobhan Lankford, Lena Corcoran, Pake Sheehan, David Neligan, Padraig O'Maidin, Sean Hyde, Timmy Kelleher, Mick Sullivan, Liam Deasy, Tom Barry, Charlie Foley, Jerh. Collins, Michael O'Brien, Dan Sando O'Donovan, Kathy Hayes, Jack Murray, Jerh. McCarthy, Anna Mulqueen, Tom Murray, Charlie O'Shea, Tom Taylor, Denis Lordan, Con Slattery, Bill McKenna, Maire Comerford, General M.J. Costello, John O'Connell, James Cahalane, Maurice Collins, Pat Murray, Jim Murray, Tim Allen, Jim Doyle, Nancy McCarthy, Maggie Sheehan, Charlie Brown, Patrick Mahony, Dan O'Callaghan, Professor Lucy Duggan, Mary O'Neill Walsh and Brother Allen.

Grateful thanks is also due to the staff at the National Library, the National Museum, the Public Records Office, the British Library Board Newspaper, to RTE Archives and the Registrars of Deaths in Cork, Ennis and Dublin.

Curly Cahalane was a tremendous help in measuring on location and drawing to scale the maps that accompany this book (Ordnance Survey maps guide). Brother Allen, Seán Kelleher, Domhnall Mac Giolla Phoil, Jim Kearney, Nellie Shannon and the Hales family, Knocknacurra gave me photos from their private collections.

Dr. T. Ryle Dwyer read the manuscript in the early stages of the work and I am sincerely grateful for his helpful suggestions. I would also like to record my thanks to Philip MacDermott and Jo O'Donoghue of Poolbeg Press.

I want to thank the many people who gave me hospitality during the course of my research, and also those who gave me information and assistance but did not wish to be named. Thanks is also due to the many who could not help directly but who took the trouble to write or telephone explaining where information could be obtained.

A special word of gratitude is due to my family, relatives and friends for their patience throughout my years of research and writing.

Any omission in this acknowledgement has not been deliberate, as the assistance of all has been gratefully appreciated.

Preface

Michael Collins was shot dead in an ambush on 22 August 1922, and in the years since then conflicting stories have been told about how he met his death. Growing up approximately 10 miles from Béal na mBláth where the ambush took place, I was well aware from an early age of the existence of these differing stories and of the passions they were capable of arousing; but it was not until 1973, when I was researching for a book on guerilla warfare in West Cork, that I became engrossed in the circumstances and the manner of Michael Collins's death.

While I was researching the War of Independence and the Civil War periods in West Cork the names of members of the Hales family of Knocknacurra, Bandon were regularly mentioned to me. Robert Hales Senior had been a man of determined Fenian opinions and his family had been amongst the first organisers of the Volunteers in West Cork. Three of his sons, Bob, Bill and Sean, fought in the crucial Crossbarry ambush on 19 March 1921, while another son Tom had been serving a jail sentence for Republican activities. Madge, a daughter, was at the same time a dispatch carrier for Michael Collins and liaised with yet another brother, Donal, an IRA supporter and journalist who was living in Italy.

Sean Hales had been in Frongoch jail with Michael Collins after the Rising of 1916. In January 1919, Collins had helped the family with the formation of the Cork No. 3 Brigade at Kilnadur, Dunmanway; by this time he had become a frequent visitor to their home. But it was a friendship that was torn in the bitter divisions that followed the signing of the Treaty. Tom Hales, Michael Collins's best friend, took the anti-Treaty side on his release from jail in December 1921 and in May 1922, Madge tried to pull de Valera from a platform in Bandon, accusing him of having tricked Collins. But the Civil War divisions were most marked on the day that Michael Collins was shot: Sean Hales, Commander of the pro-Treaty forces in West Cork, was one of the last people in Bandon to whom Michael Collins spoke before taking his fatal journey along the road where Tom Hales was amongst the Republicans who lay in ambush positions throughout the day.

When Sean Hales was shot dead a little over three months later, it was alleged that he was killed because he was investigating the death of Michael Collins. (Stories abound as to why Sean Hales was shot on 7 December 1922.)

In the course of my research for the book on guerilla warfare in West Cork I called on Neilus Flynn. During the interview he informed me that Collins had visited the Hales brothers in his house. (After the Hales's house was burned to the ground by the Black and Tans, some members of the guerilla forces stayed with the Flynns.)

This interview led to questions on Collins's death, and Neilus Flynn confessed to knowing "a Republican" who had participated in the Béal na mBláth ambush. Flynn wasn't sure if this man would grant an interview. "I'll let you know, next time you call," he said.

That man, who after some persuasion agreed to give his version of the story, was Jim Kearney. I was hooked. I had to continue investigating the death of Michael Collins and abandon my original intention of writing a book on guerilla activities in West Cork.

All the publications I encountered further fuelled the speculation as to how Collins met his death, rather than solving the mystery:

Piaras Beaslai, *Michael Collins and the Making of a New Ireland* (1926): "There are circumstances in connection with the death of Michael Collins which have never been fully cleared up."

Rex Taylor, *Michael Collins* (1958): "Rumour and

speculation are to a great extent the aids to the conversation, and the once-yearly ceremony at Béal na mBláth (the place of his death) undoubtedly reopens the topic."

Eoin Neeson, *The Civil War in Ireland* (1989): "Even today, notwithstanding the spate of recent biographical studies in newspaper articles and in book form, the facts relating to the ambush have not yet been fully gathered, evaluated and made public."

Margery Forester, *Michael Collins—The Lost Leader* (1971): "The shot that found him was almost certainly a ricochet, possibly off the armoured car."

F.S.L. Lyons, *Ireland Since the Famine* (1971): "Collins perished in an ambush laid by Irregulars, shot through the back of the head on what can only be described as a characteristically reckless expedition in which no ordinary Commander-in-Chief would have involved himself. But Collins was no ordinary man."

John M. Feehan, *The Shooting of Michael Collins — Murder or Accident?* (1981): "Michael Collins was killed in circumstances open to many different interpretations."

This is just a sample of some authors' treatment of the subject.

Because initially most of my research consisted of interviews, I accumulated numerous tape recordings and transcripts as I found I had to return many times to "key" people to clarify points. I encountered many conflicting stories, some of them bizarre. For instance, in a letter to the *Cork Examiner*, 14 September 1927, the Very Rev. P. Treacy, P.P. states that he agreed with the tenor of a speech delivered by Canon Cahalane who said: "The day Michael Collins was killed, where was de Valera? Ask the people of Béal na mBláth and they will tell you? ... The night before the murder, he slept in the immediate neighbourhood." The numerous innuendos which apportioned blame to so many people further demanded that the truth be explored, and exposed.

After I had sent several letters and made telephone calls to

Emmet Dalton, he finally agreed to grant me an interview. (Afterwards he co-operated with Cathal O'Shannon on a programme on his own life for RTE.) One interview led to another, and I was extremely fortunate in finding Billy Barry (Republican) who was involved with Jock McPeak (Free State Forces) in stealing the *Slieve na mBan* armoured car from Bandon Free State headquarters in December 1922. This led to my meeting Jim Wolfe, the driver of the armoured car on the day Michael Collins was shot. Wolfe travelled with me on the route from Limerick to Cork, and to West Cork and back to Béal na mBláth. Tim Kelleher, Collins's guide from Macroom to Bandon on that eventful morning, was my passenger on another occasion. This combination gave me an understanding of Collins's last journey, and the many stops and detours which the convoy was forced to take.

Raymond Smith of Independent Newspapers put me in touch with Jim Nicholl, in the London branch of *The Irish Independent*. These men had co-operated in writing a series of four articles in *The Irish Independent* in May 1971, based on interviews given by Jock McPeak. Jim Nicholl put me in touch with McPeak's solicitor, who in turn, told me where McPeak's wife lived; by this time, McPeak, who had spent the years following his activities in Ireland, living under an assumed name, had died in England. (I had hoped to help to fulfill Billy Barry's lifelong wish of a reunion with McPeak.)

A chance encounter at an historical conference brought me in touch with Dr. Daniel Coghlan of Crosshaven. He recommended that I see Dr. Gerard Ahern who had been a doctor in Shanakiel Hospital, where Michael Collins's body had been taken after his death. This opened another area. Dr. Gerard Ahern supplied me with documents he had obtained from Diarmuid Brennan who had spent years working on a book about Michael Collins. Brennan died before he had completed his research. Dr. Gerard also gave me names, addresses and personal letters which enabled me to get in touch with the doctors (mainly living in various parts of England) who had examined Michael Collins's body.

Meanwhile, I familiarised myself with the stones, the gaps and the ditches at Béal na mBláth. I almost haunted the place. Apart from the obvious advantage of helping me to know what those whom I interviewed were talking about, this also enabled me to gauge the credibility of individual stories.

Word of my research travelled: many times when I returned to my parents' home near Bandon, my father or some member of the family had acquired the name of a person who had requested that I call. And so my list grew.

Varied would be the best word to describe the incidents I encountered during my research—from finding myself lost on dark nights on country roads, to travelling around the Curragh Army-grounds in the *Slieve na mBan* armoured car. But, forever etched in my memory are the tears in old men's eyes, men who fought either with or against Michael Collins during the Civil War—tears of affection, of grief, and of love of a leader.

Sadly, a substantial number of men and women whom I interviewed for this book are no longer with us; however, I am happy that one of the survivors of the ambush, Jim Kearney, is still hale and hearty. Though he had kept his story from the public for many decades, he said in the course of an interview with me, in 1976, "A country—I hold—that is ashamed of its past, has no future."

Many of Michael Collins's friends who took the anti-Treaty side believed that he would not have been pro-Treaty but for his involvement in the Treaty negotiations. Certainly he felt "the split" more deeply than most. However, his personal writings are infused with hope for unity. Glad that "the foreign Power was withdrawn, the fight with the English enemy was ended," it was his belief that the duty of the Irish people was "to preserve the freedom" which they had won, because he maintained "the only way in which individual views could be rightly put forward by patriotic Irishmen was by peaceful argument and appeal." He asked, "Can we not concentrate and unite, not on the negative, but on the positive task of making a real Ireland distinct from Britain —a nation of our own?" He was convinced that there was only so much he or any leader could do, because "leaders are but individuals and individuals are imperfect, liable to error and weakness. The strength of the nation will be the strength of the whole people."

Many biographies of Michael Collins have been written, so I decided to concentrate on his final days. In the brief outline of his life in the Introduction I have made specific reference to two controversial incidents: his alleged involvement in the killing of Sir Henry Wilson and his appointment as Commander-in-Chief of the army of the Provisional Government.

The multitude of tasks which he undertook, especially following his appointment as Commander-In-Chief, would fill volumes. I have only chosen samples from his correspondence to demonstrate the complexity of his responsibilities and the circumstances which led to his death.

The affidavits which were given to me by Dr. Ned Barrett, together with Collins's correspondence in the Mulcahy papers, other papers and other sources, plus the interviews which I had with Emmet Dalton and Ernest Blythe, have all helped to place in perspective Collins's dilemma in early August. During this period he was caught between working to end the Civil War, and trying to formulate a contingency plan for the six counties.

Historian T. Ryle Dwyer has a recording of an interview given by Michael Collins's sister, Hannie, who had completed arrangements for a holiday in Ireland in August 1922. On the morning of 23 August, 1922, she arrived at work in the Kensington branch of the London Post Office. As she was about to enter her office she was stopped, taken into the superintendent's room and told that there was a rumour her brother had been killed the previous night. She was not surprised; during the night she had had a premonition about the time he was killed. "I know how unhappy he had been for so long," she said. At the moment of death "the load went ... from his mind, so it went from mine."

Because my information about the ambush has been compiled mainly from a vast number of interviews, I have not put individual reference notes in that section; I have given the names of the main contributors and listed the others in the acknowledgement pages. Many people gave me details of what happened as they saw it, only on condition that I would not manipulate their story to suit any particular slant. This I hope I have done, as I endeavoured to be fair to both the pro- and anti-Treaty sides of the conflict, and considered all the details supplied. The pieces of the jigsaw of events were sometimes hard to find, and even after finding them, often hard to place. Michael Collins became a legend in his own lifetime; because he was killed in the prime of life, that legend grew. The course which the Civil War took after his death, with the execution of prisoners, led people to speculate that if Michael Collins and Sean Hales had lived, the conduct of the war would not have sunk to such a low ebb.

Over forty-three years after Collins's death, in April 1966, Comdt. General Tom Barry (anti-Treaty) stood at Michael Collins's birthplace before an estimated 15,000 people to unveil a monument erected to the memory of the Commander-In-Chief. During his oration, Barry said, "Let us leave it that each of us, like I did myself, believed in the correctness of our choice. I concede that those who were on the opposite side believed that their decision was the right one too." Dr. Ned Barrett, who was responsible for bringing "the two sides" together on that day, could never understand why, during his youth in what he maintained was "a very Republican family," two pictures hung side by side in the living room, "one of de Valera and the other of Michael Collins." Such was the esteem of the Irish people for Collins.

One of the many surprising discoveries I made while researching the book was that Michael Collins's death has never been registered. This I found out when I tried to acquire a copy of his death certificate, to check the cause of his death.

Now, over sixty years later, his death can be registered. Michael Collins was shot dead at Béal na mBláth on 22

August 1922. The mystery of how he was shot is solved in this book, which should finally set the historical record straight.

Meda Ryan.
January 1989

Introduction

Part 1— 1890 to June 1922

Michael Collins was born on 16 October 1890 at Woodfield near Sam's Cross outside Clonakilty, Co. Cork. His father was seventy-five years old and his mother forty years younger, when Michael, the youngest of eight children, was born.

He grew up to be a strong, active child, and as the years progressed it was discovered that he was intelligent, quick-witted, quick-tempered and that he enjoyed active sport. Early in life, the brown-haired lad was made aware that he would have to find his own place in the world, that there was no money for him on the farm, but that every pair of hands was necessary for farm-work. This became more acute when his father died, just as Michael reached his sixth year.

At Lissavaird, two miles from his home, he attended school under the influential eye of Denis Lyons, a man moulded in the Fenian, nationalist tradition which he passed on to his pupils. Michael was an avid reader; he not only read but studied the writings of Thomas Davis whose works influenced his later perception of Ireland's future. By this time he was "head of his class" in Clonakilty secondary school where John Crowley was preparing him for the British Civil Service Examination. During the week-days he stayed with his married eldest sister Margaret (O'Driscoll) and the week-ends found him cycling home to Woodfield. Though he had an aptitude for figures, he much preferred the outdoor life, playing hurling and football and competing at running.

At the age of fifteen he passed the Post Office entrance examination, and in July 1906 he said goodbye to his sick mother and left Woodfield for a position as a temporary Boy-clerk in the West Kensington Post Office where his sister Hannie had been working for some years.

For the next nine and a half years he lived with Hannie in a flat over a shop at 5 Netherwood Road, West Kensington. Hannie took him to the homes of her English friends so that he would understand the people among whom he lived, and also understand their way of life.

Six months after he had left home, his mother, who had not been well for some time, died; because of job pressures and the cost involved, neither he nor Hannie was able to return for the funeral.

He soon joined the Gaelic Athletic Association (GAA) in London and played, usually, at midfield. Though not a skilled player he was dedicated and fair; his hot temper often caused him to clash all too quickly with his companions. (He was on the winning team that played a Scottish team in Liverpool in 1914.) He became secretary to the GAA's Geraldine Club in 1905 and held the post until 1915. This brought him in contact with the London Irish and introduced him to the Gaelic League classes where Irish language and Irish customs were promoted. Here he explored the stories of the Fenians (1858), who were dedicated to secure the Independence of Ireland and the establishment of an Irish Republic through physical force.

In November 1909 he was "sworn in" as a member of the Secret Society of the Irish Republican Brotherhood (IRB)[1] in Barnsbury Hall Islington, having been introduced to the Brotherhood by fellow Cork man, Sam Maguire.[2] (A leading member of the IRB, Jeremiah O'Donovan Rossa had been born "only across the fields" from Michael's Woodfield home.)

In this organisation in London, Michael found common ground with fellow countrymen with whom he enjoyed all sports, running, and jumping. He got boundless pleasure from wrestling and tussling and he became dedicated to the Irish "national cause".

During his annual holidays he stayed with his brother

Johnny and Johnny's wife Kathy at home in Woodfield. He would often be found in some neighbour's kitchen discussing the progress of the IRB and the GAA. During those long summer evenings of his two weeks holidays he once again renewed his friendship with Bob Hales, a world champion runner, and the other Hales brothers Sean, Tom and Bill. Not having been endowed with a singing voice, Michael could be relied on to recite his customary poem, "Kelly and Burke and Shea" as he stood his "full height beside the kitchen dresser" during the evening after the harvest had been threshed. And when Jerh. McCarthy, the local musician, played the barn-dance tune on his accordion, Michael gave full vent to his vigour as he whirled with one of the local girls around the kitchen.[3]

Back in London, he visited the theatre regularly and took a keen interest in painting. During these years he would sometimes be found in the company of the painter, Sir John Lavery and his good-looking wife, Lady Hazel, having been introduced to them in 1913 by Crompton Llewylen Davis. Hazel, born in America of Irish ancestry, liked Ireland and "took a deep interest in Irish affairs."[4] Through his friendship with Crompton Llewylen Davis and his wife Moira (O'Connor) Collins had become part of "the London Society Scene". Crompton Llewylen Davies was Lloyd George's solicitor at the time, and Solicitor General to the British Post Office, where previously Michael had been working in the accounts department. During this period he gleaned knowledge of Lloyd George's temperament upon which, years later, he was able to draw.

Michael, being a good conversationalist and a high spirited young man, was often invited to parties held in that circle,[5] where art, painting, and literature were discussed, and where he developed a strong friendship with Sir James Barrie, author of Peter Pan. Influenced by his circle of friends, he read the works of Dickens, H.G. Wells, Scott and George Bernard Shaw; he even confided copied extracts from Shaw's *The Man of Destiny* to his wallet. The underlining of a passage in Whitman's *Leaves of Grass* reflects his

3

philosophy at the time:

> I exist as I am, that is enough,
> If no other in the world be aware I sit content,
> And if each and all be aware I sit content.

In 1910 Michael had changed employment from the Post Office to the stockbroking firm of Horne & Co in Moorgate, and shortly afterwards to a Labour Exchange in Whitehall where he earned £70 a year. "The trade I know best is the financial trade, but from study and observation I have acquired a wider knowledge of social and economic conditions and have specially studied the building trade and unskilled labour."[6] As he became competent at typewriting, a further period found him working in the London office of the Guarantee Trust Company of New York.

Early in 1914, he wrote in a personal notebook:

"However happy I happen to be in a particular job, the thought is always with me that my future is otherwise than among the facts and figures of money. Yet I do not dream of greater things...only the thought is always there."[7]

Perhaps it was this thought that sparked off the idea of enrolling as an Irish Volunteer in No. 1 Company, London on 25 April, 1914. He was then 24 years of age. Forthwith he began his weekly contributions towards the purchase of a rifle. His drilling with the company took place in a German gymnasium at King's Cross and as with all his activities he endeavoured to give of his best.

August of that year saw the outbreak of the Great War. Talks of conscription began. And in England many Irish, when faced with this prospect, began to return home. By this time Michael had been promoted to the position of treasurer of the IRB for London and the South of England.

Towards the end of the year, he had considered joining his brother Patrick in Chicago, but first decided to take a short trip to Dublin. Through the IRB, he contacted Tom Clarke and Sean MacDiarmada. After his first meeting with them he had decided on his future. His return to London was brief.

On 15 January 1916, he left his sister's flat at Kensington, (after the British Government had introduced a certain compulsory military service) and journeyed back to Ireland. Back in Dublin, he found employment with Craig, Gardner & Co. Accountants; here he became friendly with Joe McGrath, who was later to become his "right-hand" intelligence man. In the evenings he became heavily involved in the work of the IRB and the Volunteers, where at Larkfield Manor training camp in Kimmage, he perfected his shot in preparation for the Rising which took place in Dublin on Easter Monday 1916.

Staff Captain Michael Collins served as aide-de-camp to Joseph Plunkett, one of the leaders of the Rising. He was near the front rank of the group that seized the GPO. When the exhausted Plunkett, who was ill, went upstairs to rest during the fighting, Collins took his turn at the operations' table in the main office. Despite the confusion he efficiently plotted positions in other parts of the city on a map and kept the Commanding Officers informed about reports brought in by Cumann na mBan.

While in charge of the instrument room below the parapeted roof of the GPO, the section of the building that got the greatest shelling from British artillery, he found the heat from the flames intense. Yet, showing no fear, he struggled through flames, and constantly praised the men under his command for their gallantry. Under sniping and gunfire the men held the building until Saturday afternoon when various parts of it were ablaze.

Collins was among the weary men who had to throw down their guns and were led to the lawn of the Rotunda hospital. There he spent that night with the group under military guard. The following morning the prisoners, cold and miserable, were marched under heavy military escort to Richmond Barracks.

A light-hearted and humorous young man, Collins went into the Rising as if to satisfy his restless spirit and savour his first experience of war. He enjoyed the prestige of soldering: he was cool and efficient; he had set himself a challenge and was determined to achieve honour. Soon he learned that war was no game, that he would have to accept defeat and humiliation, and witness suffering. His character was being shaped by the bitter experience of the Rising and by his arrest. Some of his fellow Volunteers would, over the weeks ahead, face the firing squad,[8] while he and others would be imprisoned.

He was one of 238 men shipped from Dublin docks to the detention barracks at Stafford on 1 May 1916, and listed as "Irish Prisoner 48F."[9] Three weeks of solitary confinement were followed by the prisoners being allowed to see each other briefly in the exercise yard of Stafford prison. The end of June found Collins in one of the British internment camps in Frongoch, North Wales. Here two important factors structured his future. First, he formed friendships with men of similar ideas and ideals. Secondly, he advanced his learning by studying the Irish language and English literature. His friendships, his knowledge, his determination, and his ability to think clearly—all these contributed to his leadership qualities and earned him the nickname "The Big Fellow."

Fellow Corkman Sean Hales who became his greatest friend was to play an important part in Collins's life during the Civil War. An athlete and sportsman, he was often found wrestling with Collins. The two strong-willed men could be found tussling with each other in the exercise yard, with neither giving in, until exhaustion would demand that they call it quits.

Collins was among the untried prisoners who were released unconditionally, in December 1916. He was happy to return to Clonakilty and he walked the last few miles to Woodfield. When he went in the door on Christmas night he found his family and neighbours "waking" his grandmother whom he loved, and who had died the previous night. Over the following three weeks he sampled the feelings of the people in his native locality and compared these with his own. He discovered that since the Rising and the executions, local volunteer bodies, who had been meeting at centres throughout West Cork, had become more determined to achieve their objective by physical force.

Back in Dublin in January 1917, Michael Collins found lodgings at 44 Mountjoy Street, which was to be his base over the next few years. His appointment as secretary and accountant of the Amalgamated National Aid Association and Volunteer Dependants' Fund earned him a wage of £2/10s a week. Working at 10 Exchequer Street, he gained important experience which was helpful in his IRB activities later. According to Joe McGrath he was extremely methodical, "a ball of fire, very quick on the uptake, rarely if ever, missing a point and a good listener where learning the job was concerned."

His capacity for work impressed all who came in contact with him. Being extremely methodical, but quick tempered, he would sometimes have little patience with those who did not see his point of view. He liked to joke and sometimes swore with a variety of expletives followed by a loud burst of laughter.

At this stage it was becoming clear that he had decided to devote his life to the nationalist cause. With the aid of Ned Broy, an employee of Dublin Castle, Collins began to build a highly professional and successful intelligence network which was eventually to crack the British espionage system in Ireland. In February 1917 he was co-opted to the Supreme Council of the IRB, and with Sam Maguire he made periodic trips to London to organise a system of "gun-running." Shortly after the death of his friend, Thomas Ashe[10] (who died in Mountjoy jail after a period of "forced feeding"), Collins was appointed secretary of the Supreme Council of the IRB and thus a member of the three-man standing Executive.

In Sligo, in April 1918 Collins was arrested for making a speech in which he told the people to resist the conscription which the British Government intended to enforce on the Irish people. He was the first to jump bail and "go on the run," a decision which was to become policy for the movement. He successfully evaded capture for the duration of the War of Independence.

In the 1918 general election he was returned as Sinn Féin

member for South Cork and took his seat in the first Dáil in January 1919. He was appointed Minister of Home Affairs and later, as Minister of Finance, was responsible for organising a successful National loan. He continued to be an active member of the IRB Executive and in mid-1919 he became President of the Supreme Council, a post which he held until his death.[11] By now Volunteers were being trained throughout the country and ambushes, raids and arrests were taking place—what was later called the War of Independence.

The British intelligence structure was efficient and powerful with vast resources and a reputation for invincibility, yet within a few years Collins had broken it. He created his own spectacular system which monitored British military planning. His men sorted mail in post offices throughout the county; they were porters in hotels, ticket collectors in railway stations, workers in factories, dockers in ports and warders in prisons. In the Post Office, Collins's cousin Nancy O'Brien arranged for decoded messages to be sent to him. In important military centres around the country he had men and women who supplied information; many ordinary people were the eyes and ears that aided Collins's network. Furthermore, he tabulated material received from four key men who infiltrated G-Division of Dublin Castle (Joe Kavanagh, James MacNamara, Ned Broy and Dave Neligan.) In the second half of 1919 when the war against the British intensified, Collins structured a special "Squad" made up of twelve men who were given the task of eliminating key members of British Intelligence.

In early October 1920 a special group of British officers with Secret Service training (under Col. Sir Arthur Winter) arrived in Ireland hoping to crack Collins's network. They mingled with some of the G-men in the Castle, but mainly they posed as business men, and were dubbed "The Cairo gang" not because they had anything to do with Cairo (as has always been believed) but because they frequented a pub known as The Cairo.[12]

Through Collins's intelligence system detailed information was obtained about them, and in a simultaneous attack on their homes, digs and guesthouse accommodation, in a pre-dawn raid on 21 November 1920, The Squad shot dead eleven British Intelligence agents.[13] This provoked a reprisal: lorry-loads of British forces invaded Croke Park that afternoon while a football match between Tipperary and Dublin was in progress, firing indiscriminately on the players and the crowd. Twelve people died and sixty were wounded.

Collins, meanwhile, rode around Dublin on an old rusty bicycle. He attended meetings in various pubs and venues, often avoiding capture by seconds. Once, when his office was being raided, he heard men coming to the door so he handed his revolver to his secretary and gathered up a bundle of papers. He went to the window but discovered there was no down-pipe, so he bustled past the men at the door, went up one flight of stairs and out through the skylight. He remained on the roof-top until the raid was over.

Many instances have been recorded where Collins narrowly avoided being captured. Twice on Christmas Eve 1920, he evaded the police. Early in the night, he had asked for a private room in the Gresham Hotel for a meeting with some of his men, but none was available. As the men made their way to the main dining room they were stopped by a group of Auxiliaries. Collins, though caught with an Ordnance Survey map in his pocket, bluffed his way out, went with his companions to Vaughan's Hotel (one of his regular haunts) and had only just left that premises when the place was raided.

During this period while de Valera was in America collecting funds, Collins was a regular visitor to the de Valera family home in Greystones, lending moral support to Sinéad.

While "on the run" he stayed in a Longford hotel owned by the Kiernans. He became friendly with the attractive Kitty Kiernan and soon a romance developed. In times of separation she wrote to him constantly, and he responded often, sometimes with brief notes. (Their prolific letter-writing during the short period of their association has filled a book entitled *In Great Haste*, edited by Leon O'Broin.)

In Collins's native West Cork during this period, the guerilla campaign had been notably successful under the leadership of such men as Tom Barry and Liam Deasy. In mid-May 1921 Collins decided that he would like to discuss the campaign with Tom Barry, Commander of the Third West Cork Flying Column—this was mainly because Barry had been pressing Collins at GHQ for more armaments. When they met, Barry informed Collins that more arms and ammunition were urgently needed in order to step up the campaign so that the British government would be pressurised into a surrender situation. Donal Hales, a journalist in Italy,[14] with whom Collins was in constant contact, was in the process of securing a shipment of armaments which was to land near Union Hall in West Cork. Though a big planning operation was undertaken by the IRA in West Cork in preparation for the armament, this shipment did not materalise. And by mid-1921 events seemed to be closing in on Collins. Dave Neligan was the only "inside" intelligence man left in the Castle and he told Collins "things are getting hot." Furthermore, a bid to rescue the jailed Sean MacEoin, leader of the Longford Flying Column, failed. Almost in despair Collins wrote: "Cork will be fighting alone."[15]

Yet, pleas for arms by the three Cork Brigades were useless. Collins and GHQ were powerless. Collins told de Valera, "unless the boys get arms and ammunition, it's all over." He decided to make one more effort and sent Madge Hales over to her brother in Italy; she was to report back to Collins on the position.[16]

It had reached the stage where further resistance was proving increasingly difficult for Collins. Cracks had begun to appear in his intelligence system and he began to doubt whether the Volunteers could hold out for very much longer as an effective force.[17] Madge Hales arrived back from Italy in June 1921 and informed Collins that only half a boat-load of armaments could be obtained, and other difficulties meant that the anticipated arms shipment to Ireland was postponed again.[18]

Talks of a Truce were imminent, and on 11 July a Truce was announced which was welcomed not alone by Collins but by all of the the IRA.

In Collins's native county the three Cork Brigades hoped it would be a short truce and that a fresh supply of ammunition would soon make it possible for them to renew the fight. However, these men felt they should have been consulted, especially because Collins had shown his appreciation of their intensive fighting.[19] It appears that seeds of discontent were sown at this period which were to spring to life later.

Collins was aware of the failure to obtain munitions and how this very serious shortage hampered the fight, "because men, no matter how determined they may be, or how courageous cannot fight with their bare hands."[20] Yet, he did not inform any of the Brigades of the difficulties he had encountered in the acquisition of the Italian arms shipment and so the information remained within GHQ. This was a mistake on Collins's part which later was to create many enemies for him.

By this time de Valera made it known that he was prepared to talk to Lloyd George and subsequently received an invitation to London.

Following intensive Dail debates, it was decided that Collins should be among the five-man delegation led by Aurther Griffith, who would travel to London to negotiate Treaty settlement terms. Collins was reluctant to accept this responsibility. He maintained that by remaining at home he would be in a stronger position to influence Republicans towards a compromise settlement, which all felt sure would be the outcome. But De Valera argued that Collins was vital to the delegation.[21]

Speaking in the Dail, Collins said, "To me the task is a loathsome one. If I go, I go in the spirit of a soldier who acts against his judgement at the orders of a superior officer."[22] But de Valera could not be dissuaded; and when Cathal Brugha and Austin Stack refused to go, Collins accepted the responsibility. "I had no choice," he said, " I had to go."[23]

On Saturday 8 October 1921, before his departure for

London, he became unofficially engaged to his girl friend Kitty Kiernan from Granard, Co. Longford. They would keep in touch, they would write to each other, and he would be home periodically. The first meeting of the delegation took place in London on 11 October 1921. Throughout the period of negotiations, he wrote to Kitty regularly. Mostly it was just a few lines letting her know how he felt about the progress of the negotiations and some personal words. In mid-November he telegraphed her to visit him. With her sister she made the trip to London in November. One day Michael asked Kathleen Napoli McKenna, one of the secretaries, to accompany the Kiernan sisters on a shopping expedition. They each were to select a gift for which he would pay. Kitty selected a smart woollen dress. Kathleen McKenna said, "Mick, who was very much in love with Kitty, was a proud man as he left Cadogan Gardens with one of the sisters in each arm." (Their engagement was not officially announced until after the Treaty ratification.)

Collins was an able negotiator. During one of the committee meetings in the London debates Churchill was arguing some carefully prepared points while the Irish delegation remained silent. "Have you any answer to these?" Collins scribbled on a note to Emmet Dalton.

"No," came Dalton's reply.

Having listened a while longer, Collins suddenly became exasperated and slammed his fist on the table. "For Christ's sake, come to the point."

Churchill sat speechless. While he still had a stunned expression Collins erupted into an infectious laugh which Churchill, in spite of himself, soon joined, thereby dissipating much of the force of his carefully prepared case.[24]

In the afternoon of 5 December 1921 Lloyd George held up two envelopes saying: "Here are the alternative letters which I have prepared ... we must have your answer by 10 pm. tonight. You can have until then, but no longer, to decide whether you will give peace or war to your country."[25]

When the delegation withdrew, "Michael Collins rose, looking as though he was going to shoot someone. I have never seen so much pain and suffering in restraint," wrote Winston Churchill.

Late that evening Collins visited his friends Sir John and Lady Hazel Lavery at 5 Cromwell Place. He was extremely angry that pressure was being brought to bear on him, because he disagreed with aspects of the Treaty. Sir John failed to dissuade him when he "lost his temper." But eventually "after hours of persuasion" Hazel succeeded in calming him. Then "She took him to Downing Street in her car that last evening, and he gave in," Sir John wrote.[26]

Collins was reluctant to embroil Ireland in a further war. He knew more than any member of the delegation how his efforts to obtain further arms had failed. He was aware as he wrote afterwards that the alternative to the Treaty "sooner or later" was war, and aware also that "what we fought for at any particular time was the greatest measure of freedom obtainable at that time … "[27]

At 2.20 on the morning of 6 December, both sides signed the "Articles of Agreement for a treaty between Great Britain and Ireland." Afterwards, when Birkenhead said, "I may have signed my political death-warrant tonight," Collins replied, "I may have signed my actual death-warrant."[28]

After signing the Treaty on 6 December 1921, Collins went back to the Laverys where he was able to relax after a difficult day's bargaining. Then he returned to his lodgings in the early hours of the morning and went to bed. Though he regarded the Treaty as "the first real step for Ireland," deep down he was aware that many of his friends both in the Volunteers and in the Dáil would not accept his explanation.

He could not rest so he got up and in a letter to his friend, John O'Kane asked: "Will anyone be satisfied at the bargain?" He could visualise the disturbance that was about to erupt. He was writing his obituary because he told O'Kane he had signed his own death warrant: "a bullet might just have done the job five years ago."[29]

It was a disturbed Collins who returned to Ireland to face the Dáil questioning.

He never hid the fact that he disliked politics and was

much more at ease while working on intelligence and soldiering. "To be a politician one needs to keep tongue in cheek for all of the day and most of the night; one needs to have the ability to say one thing and mean another; one needs to be abnormally successful at the art of twisting the truth," he wrote. "Can you wonder that I think and think, yet never manage to achieve peace of mind? It is more than possible that one's words will be taken out of context, twisted, warped, shaped into a lie, and be flung back into my teeth."[30]

Back in the Dáil in Dublin, after some intense discussion and often bitter remarks, the Treaty motion was carried by seven votes on 7 January 1922.[31] Subsequently, de Valera resigned as President of the Republic and Arthur Griffith was elected in his place. Griffith appointed a cabinet which included Collins as Minister of Finance. The ratification of the Treaty opened the way for the formation of a Provisional Government which assembled on 14 January. Michael Collins was elected Chairman.

Political confusion reigned as Griffith and his temporary government endeavoured to complete the business of the Second Dáil and Collins and his Provisional Government proceeded to take over power in the area encompassing the Twenty-Six Counties as constituted by the 1920 Government of Ireland Act. Control of the Six Counties rested with Stormont.

As army barracks were being evacuated by the British military they were being replaced by either pro- or anti-Treaty men depending on the area or the circumstances. Military men who declared for acceptance of the Treaty were armed, uniformed and paid by the Provisional Government, thus forming the nucleus of the "National" army (later The Free State Army), with headquarters at Beggar's Bush. Anti-Treaty men like Liam Lynch, Rory O'Connor, Tom Barry and others regarded this as a betrayal of Mulcahy's undertaking that the IRA would be maintained as the Army of the Republic. The seeds of a military struggle were being sown.

An air of hostility began to emerge throughout the country

as anti-Treatyites began to make their presence felt. Despite the Dáil cabinet's prohibition, an army convention was held on 26 March with the intention of renewing the army's allegiance to the Republic. The result of this convention was a split in the army. An Executive and an Army Council with Liam Lynch as Chief of Staff were formed. This meant there were two armies in the country, one loyal to the Provisional government and the other to the Republican Executive. On 14 April Rory O'Connor seized the Four Courts as headquarters despite Liam Lynch's opposition. This act was seen by Churchill as a major act of defiance against the Provisional Government. Collins and Richard Mulcahy (Minister of Defence) were reluctant to act against former comrades, and did everything possible to avoid open confrontation.

Ironically, Collins and Lynch continued to work together in sending arms to the North. At this stage, they wanted to help Northern Catholics who were the victims of pograms. Because the guns that came from the British supplies would be too easily identified, Collins insisted that the Executive men (anti-Treatyites) should supply an agreed number of rifles towards "the Northern operation." Beggar's Bush (Army of Provisional Government) then replaced these with an equal number of British-supplied weapons. Both the Executive and Beggar's Bush co-operated in supplying men for an offensive which began in Belfast on 18 May 1922. Even after the Army split, both sides (Lynch and Collins to the fore) had a common policy which they continued to operate jointly, though two separate Army commands had been structured.[32] This shows that Collins was prepared to work with his opponents to undermine one aspect of the Treaty, while supporting the Treaty in public. He was well aware of the ambiguity of this situation.

During the early months of 1922 IRB conferences continued to be held in an effort to save the organisation from splitting on the Treaty issue. Though Collins and Lynch were the principal protagonists in the opposing sides, each respected the other's apparent immovable position; there was a sense of brotherhood born out of their intimate association during the War of Independence. However, as president of the Supreme Council, Collins succeeded in getting the organisation to accept the Treaty. This led inevitably to further conflict.

At a Republican Executive convention held on 18 June, Tom Barry proposed that instead of further discussion on Army reunification the convention should give an ultimatum to the British Government to withdraw their troops within seventy-two hours.[33] He wanted to renew the war with Britain and hoped that this would unite the army. When Lynch, Deasy and Moylan disagreed, a split occurred on the issue; Joseph McKelvey was voted to replace Lynch as Chief-of-Staff of the Executive; Tom Barry, Rory O'Connor and Liam Mellows left to occupy the Four Courts.

An election was held in June 1922 and despite the existence of a pact between de Valera and Collins that was to rule out confrontation between Treatyites and anti-Treatyites, the vote turned out to be an expression of the people's views on the Treaty. The election results announced on 24 June, showed that out of one hundred and twenty-eight seats, fifty-eight pro-Treaty candidates were elected and thirty-five were anti-Treaty (plus thirty-five others). Collins was later accused of sabotaging the pact.

Events were gaining momentum. The political atmosphere created by the Treaty division was now cemented by the failure of the Pact, and the collapse of the attempt at Army reunification.

Part 11—June to August 1922

In London, Reginald Dunne and Joseph O'Sullivan of the IRA's London battalion assassinated Field Marshall Sir Henry Wilson, Military Adviser to the Six County Administration, on 22 June 1922. Dunne and O'Sullivan were arrested.

The British ministers incorrectly blamed the Four Courts garrison for the killing, believing that they had ordered the assassination. Rory O' Connor made a public statement that he had nothing to do with the killing. "If we had, we would admit it." It has been alleged that Collins ordered or consented to the killing, yet this has never been established; because he had given an order for the assassination in pre-Treaty days, it has been suggested that this was never cancelled. But Joe Dolan of Collins's old intelligence group said that Collins instructed Sam Maguire O/C Britain during the Anglo-Irish War to carry out the execution; Maguire, he said, carried out the order by asking "Dunne O/C London to do the job." Margery Forester in *The Lost Leader* states: "Collins was not a man who absent-mindedly left execution orders unrevoked. It is infinitely more probable that far from doing so, he renewed the order to Dunne shortly before it was carried out when the Belfast pogroms were at their height."[1]

It is true that, angered by the frequent and futile murders of Catholics in the north, Collins insisted that it was the duty of the British Government and particularly that of Wilson (whom he mistrusted) to restore order in the north of Ireland. By now he believed northern events were moving towards a state of conflict in which the south would become involved thus wrecking the Treaty, and his "stepping stone" policy.

However, Collins agreed with Griffith's assessment of the

killing of Wilson that: "It is a fundamental principle of civilised government that the assassination of a political opponent cannot be justified or condoned."

Regardless of whether or not Collins had any knowledge of, or any involvement in, Wilson's death, he took full responsibility for the lives of Dunne and O'Sullivan; he sent Tom Cullen to London to see if they could be freed or if there were any escape possibilities. All of Collins's plans to rescue the two men were futile, having proved impracticable, even his bizarre scheme to have a distinguished British person taken and held as a hostage.[2]

When the London Government placed blame for the killing on the anti-Treaty forces in the Four Courts, Collins searched for a way out of the dilemma. "He paced the floor, hurried out to see Tim Healy about legal counsel for their trial, and brushed aside other pressing business even from close colleagues with the curt rejoinder that Dunne and O'Sullivan were more important."[3]

Ernest Blythe was present when Griffith and Collins jointly formulated a statement of condemnation for the press. Watching and listening to the two men, Blythe formed the impression, "that though Collins was as disturbed as Griffith was, he had more information about it than his senior colleague ... But that does not mean that he was involved. The London branch [IRB] could have decided ... perhaps they had their own motives" for killing Wilson.[4]

Despite publicly condemning the assassination Collins's "dualism" had him privately seeking rescue methods. The event led to emergency cabinet meetings being held in London; though the British could not prove any connection between the shooting of Wilson and the IRA in the Four Courts, suspicion was deep because documents were found on Dunne and O'Sullivan which referred to an IRA scheme and the need for organisation in London.[5]

Mentally Collins was in a state of torture. Blythe remembers him being irritable while he searched for a "loophole." He gave the impression that "he didn't want his former colleagues who were in the Four Courts to be blamed in the wrong, even though they were fast becoming his military enemies."[6]

Despite all Collins's efforts to free the men, Dunne and O'Sullivan were tried at the Old Bailey on 18 July, 1922, found guilty and sentenced to death.[7] Nevertheless as the days moved on Collins was still troubled. Mr McDonnell of London sent him a "note of the evidence at the appeal" and arising from this Collins wrote to Cosgrave: "I am of the opinion that we must now make an official representation that mercy be extended to these men. Please let me know what is being done in the matter."[8]

Collins's letter was discussed at a Provisional Government meeting "and it was decided that official representations should be made to the British Government on behalf of these men."[9] The Law Officer prepared another appeal which was unsuccessful. The law took its course.

Despite Collins's allegiance to his colleagues in the Provisional Government and the honouring of the Treaty signature, he was, up to this period engaged in a dualist approach, especially in his activities relating to the Northern operation. His method was to placate both of the divisions which resulted from the Army split. Moreover he continued his membership of the IRB (secret organisation) together with Lynch. Reginald Dunne was also a member of this organisation. He had not actively either opposed or supported the implementation of the Treaty, but like Sam Maguire he was great friends with Collins since their London IRB days. So whether the assassination of Wilson which was planned by the London IRB network was carried out under Collins's orders or taken on by Dunne to win favour with Collins or in the hope of uniting the Army to a common purpose is a debatable point.

Collins's attempt to seek a reprieve for Dunne and O'Sullivan does not necessarily mean that he had ordered the killing of Wilson; his concern might only have meant that he wanted to secure his friends' freedom. Moreover, he was, during this period, still communicating with the anti-Treatyites. There is much speculation about an alleged order

19

by Collins. However, Dunne's anger expressed to Bill Aherne the week before the killing does not bear out the allegation.

Bill Aherne (an anti-Treaty supporter) told Ulick O'Connor that he (Aherne) "met Reggie Dunne in Dublin a week before the affair and he remembered clearly how angry Dunne was that Collins would not allow him proceed with the killing."[10] Furthermore, Collins spoke to Emmet Dalton during a visit to Portobello Barracks a few days after the shooting of Wilson about a modus operandi in connection with Dunne and O'Sullivan. The possibility of organising an escape was discussed. These men were Collins's friends. According to Dalton, Collins was angry that the London IRA had taken an irresponsible attitude "at this time"—this was a day or two prior to the decision to shell the Four Courts. "Collins had enough of problems around this period; he was hoping that army reunification was still a possibility," said Dalton. "Therefore, I do not believe that Collins ordered the shooting of Wilson at this time ... Any orders prior to the Truce were revoked when the Truce was declared."[11]

Whoever ordered or decided on the shooting of Sir Henry Wilson by Dunne and O'Sullivan on 22 June 1922, the event brought matters swiftly to a head.

On the day Wilson was shot Lloyd George wrote to Collins "to inform" him "that documents have been found upon the murderers" which "reveal the existence of a definite conspiracy against the peace and order of this country." Other information revealed "that active preparations are on foot among the irregular elements of the IRA to resume attacks upon the lives and property of British subjects both in England and in Ulster." Lloyd George was no longer prepared to permit Rory O'Connor "to remain with his followers and his arsenal in open rebellion in the heart of Dublin in possession of the Courts of Justice ... " so on behalf of "His Majesty's Government" he felt "entitled" to ask Collins to "formally" bring "to an end" this "state of things." Furthermore, he was prepared to place at Collins's disposal "the necessary pieces of artillery which may be required."[12]

Whatever Collins's involvement in the death of Wilson, he took full responsibility and yielded to British pressure. On 24 June, Macready, still in command of the remnant of British forces in Dublin, received orders to attack the Four Courts the following day.[13] While he was preparing to carry out orders the British Cabinet altered its decision, and in agreement with Macready cancelled its instructions; instead Churchill, speaking in the House of Commons on 26 June gave the Provisional Government an ultimatum. Unless they brought the occupation of the Four Courts to a speedy end, the Treaty would be regarded as having been violated and so "full liberty of action" would be resumed.

The other issue that made the storming of the Four Courts inevitable was the holding (as hostage) of pro-Treaty deputy Chief-of-Staff, J.J. (Ginger) O'Connell by Executive Forces. He was held in order to secure the release of Leo Henderson who had been arrested by Provisional Government troops whilst on the point of commandeering transport for the removal of supplies to the north—a project on which both sides (Collins's men/Lynch's men) were still nominally co-operating. Collins's dualism had to stop.

"It was decided" by him and by the Provisional Government at an emergency meeting that "Notices should be served on the armed men in illegal occupation of the Four Courts and Fowles Hall that night ordering them to evacuate the buildings, and to surrender up all arms and property." Should they refuse to comply with this order then Collins was determined that "the necessary military action would be taken at once."[14]

Blythe believed that in agreeing to British pressure to lay siege to the anti-Treaty forces in the Four Courts, Collins hoped that those inside would surrender, and as a consequence the lives of Dunne and O'Sullivan who were awaiting execution, could be saved.[15]

Liam Lynch visited the Four Courts on the night of 27 June. Here the split in the Republican garrison was healed and Lynch resumed his position as Chief-of-Staff. Ernest Blythe said that the cabinet members believed "they were still split when we laid siege to the Four Courts. Collins estimated that because Lynch was not with them, our task would be easy."[16]

On Wednesday 28 June, an ultimatum delivered to the Four Courts's garrison to surrender before 4 a.m. yielded no response. At 4.07 a.m. two eighteen-pounder guns borrowed from the British Army opened fire on the building and so the Civil War officially began. By Friday, 30 June the Republican garrison had surrendered unconditionally. Churchill was pleased and sent a congratulatory telegram to Collins.

The day of reckoning had arrived for Collins. He would now have to be prepared to fight openly against his friends. Lynch, Deasy and a number of the Republican Executive, who were in the Clarence Hotel across the river from the Four Courts when the attack opened, issued a hurried proclamation calling on the Republican army to resume the fight for the Republic. They made their way south, where the area south of a line stretching from Waterford to Limerick was to be held by the Republicans. Oscar Traynor took command in Dublin, where, during that week sporadic skirmishes caused much destruction.

At a meeting of the Provisional Government on 1 July, Collins announced that Richard Mulcahy, Minister of Defence, had transferred to Portobello Barracks, and had taken over command, and that he himself would act as Minister of Defence for the present. Also "the Minister of Labour Mr McGrath had taken up duties in the same barracks …"[17]

On 3 July, at a Government meeting it was decided that "the Army should be increased by a Volunteer Force, up to an extra 20,000 men levied throughout the country to serve for a period of six months," at an estimated cost of £3,000,000.[18]

Problems were mounting for Collins. Demanding decisions had to be made daily.

During early July, anti-Treaty forces constantly clashed with Government forces, and it looked as though the Government, the Treaty and all that Collins had worked for, were swiftly being eroded. Sporadic fighting had begun to

22

spread throughout various parts of the country, and as most of the military barracks and the main cities and towns were in the hands of Republican forces, it was time to act. Matters discussed at Government meetings concerned military decisions rather than political issues. Collins needed to get a grip of the problems. He would go back to soldiering and take command. He wrote to Griffith pointing out the priority required for military matters, suggesting that the government should issue "a sort of official instruction" on the formation of a War Council and appoint him as Commander-in-Chief.[19]

So, at a Government meeting on Wednesday 12 July, Collins "announced that he had arranged to take up duty as Commander in Chief of the army and would not be able to act in his ministerial capacity until further notice, and that Messrs. O'Higgins, McGrath and Fionan Lynch had also been appointed to military posts." At this meeting W.T. Cosgrave, Minister of Local Government, "was appointed to act as chairman of the Provisional Government and as Minister of Finance in the absence of Mr. Collins on military duties." There was agreement "that Parliament should be prorogued for a further fortnight, to meet on Saturday 29th instant, and that an official proclamation should be issued to that effect."[20]

A further meeting held later in the day dealt with the establishment of the Civic Guards and the proroguing of parliament, before moving on to the discussion on the military situation. The Civil War was raging so this was the important matter. Collins was clearly commander of the military situation since the morning meeting. At this meeting three men were appointed to form a War Council: "Michael Collins—General Commander-in-Chief; Richard Mulcahy—General Chief of Staff and Minister of Defence. Eoin O'Duffy—General in Command South-Western Division."[21]

In recent years it has been alleged that Michael Collins was ousted from his position as Chairman of the Provisional Government and given the job as Commander-In-Chief of the Army in order to reduce his political power. But the note in his diary on the 12 July, does not support this argument.

"At Gov. meeting this evening Council of War appointed, M.C. C in C; R.J.M. M.D. & C of S; G.O'D. C of S & G.O.C. South W. Command."[22]

This is an abbreviated version by Collins recording the meeting and using the word "appointed."

From Collins's correspondence at this period it is obvious that his principal aim was to get the country back to stability. As soon as he got into his office in Portobello Barracks he set about organising the army,[23] organising reconnissance[24] to monitor the activities of the anti-Treaty forces, and organising his "Immediate Objective"[25] of sending officers with men into each area. He wanted details of arms captured or surrendered;[26] he commanded that garrisons be strengthened;[27] he ordered commanders to take towns and to move on with their men,[28] he wanted lists of vehicles taken over from the British,[29] and ships should be prepared for the transportation of troops by sea.[30]

Clearly from the day he took over as Commander-In-Chief he fulfilled the role of General Commanding-In-Chief (title conferred on him)[31] for the Army of the Provisional Government.

The official letter sent to Collins and signed by members of the Provisional Government stated: "You have been entrusted with the Supreme Command of the National Army and with General Mulcahy and General O'Duffy you have been constituted a War Council to direct the military operations now in progress ...[32] (See Appendix 11).

The Irish Times carried a leading article on Collins's appointment as Commander-in-Chief, regarding it as "a wise move ... everything must be done that is essential to deal with the heavy task that lies before the National force in the South and portions of the West."[33]

So, temporarily relieved of Ministerial duties, Collins moved into quarters at Portobello Barracks.[34] In many of his letters he addressed Cosgrave as "Acting Chairman" or "Acting Minister of Finance" depending on the contents. Cosgrave wrote to Collins as "Commander in Chief" or "General Commanding in Chief" and on some occasions addressed him as "Chairman" depending on the letter. On a few occasion Collins signed himself under the style of "Chairman"[35] and still regarded himself as such; however, his task at this period was to safeguard the stability of the country.

The administration of the National Army was a substantial responsibility. It would take time to organise the distribution of payment, food supplies and clothing to scattered groups of soldiers constantly on the move. Tirelessly, Collins worked into the night hours at his Portobello desk.[36] His notebook of those July days bears witness to the urgency with which he tackled most tasks and the number of items that crowded upon him. There were prison accommodation, medical service, engineering, press data, intelligence lists and a multitude of other concerns.

Clearly Collins was back on familiar ground, endeavouring to put behind him the arena of politics and concentrate all his energies on the military aspect. When Churchill wrote concerning political matters, Collins responded, " ... Since I have been entrusted with supreme command of the National Army, I have scarcely a moment for any business other than the urgent business of restoring peace and settled conditions to the country."[37] Collins was concerned that the situation for Catholics in the north of Ireland was deteriorating and felt that the restoration of order was vital. Consequently, he said in a letter to Churchill that "were it not for my new obligations and commitments I would be devoting all available time and energy towards its solution."[38]

He sought and obtained support from the Government to make certain "political" decisions,[39] and he allotted to Dalton the task of recruiting men from "the Legion of Irish Ex-Servicemen."[40]

Collins maintained that the majority of the Irish people accepted the Treaty. It was agonising for him that "the good fighting men from Cork" were his "opponents" but he hoped that without the support of the people they would "soon realize they have no hope,"[41] because in this Civil War the men "have died and are suffering for the very same principle that we fought the British for ..."[42]

He left the lines of communication open, and was willing to talk to mediators, yet his primary objective was to get Republican-held areas under Provisional Government control and to stop the seizure of money from banks[43] and other revenue sources, thus suffocating the opposition before they could gain a secure foothold.

Having received reports that intensive organisation was being undertaken by the anti-Treaty leaders and reports also that they were gaining support in County Cork, Collins felt this could only be counteracted by co-ordinating the National troops and using the tactics of "a sudden swoop."

The sadness of Civil War is felt most when life-long friends become bitter enemies or when brothers and neighbours take opposite sides; indeed Collins found the heart-break of friends deciding to take the opposing viewpoint a piercing reality. This was brought clearly home to him when his friend Harry Boland was shot by Government forces while being taken prisoner on the night of 31 July; it marked a moment of truth.

In a letter to his girl friend Kitty Kiernan, he mentioned seeing a small crowd outside St Vincent's Hospital:

"My mind went into his lying dead there and I thought of the times together ... Although the gap of 8 or 9 months was not forgotten—of course no one can ever forget it—I only thought of him with the friendship of the days of 1918 and 1919."[44]

Yet for Collins, duty came first. He asked the Director of Intelligence to place a guard on St. Vincent's Hospital "and to make a report on the exact condition of Mr. Harry Boland," and to find out "whether he has been operated on and what the doctors think of his condition."[45] When Boland died Collins gave the names of people who were "at the Inquest" to the Director of Intelligence because "they all made speeches about murder" and he wanted them to be watched.[46]

A couple of days later he asked Acting Major General Tobin to "detail a few men with some sort of a party to attend the Curragh races to see whether any of the Irregulars we want, attend. If there are any of them they could be put into the Curragh Camp temporarily."[47]

His former friends were now enemies and should be spied on.[48] Such was the bitter twist required to win this Civil War, and the painful reality for Collins. But by the first week in August he had decided there would be no compromise; his opponents had no intention of yielding and this brought forth his true determination.[49]

"In the south, the immediate military problem that confronts us," he wrote, "is not so much the military defeat of the Irregulars in that area as the establishing of our Forces in certain principal points in the area, with a view to shaking the domination held over the ordinary people by the Irregulars."[50]

John L. O'Sullivan remembers Collins being in high spirits when he discussed a method of taking the West Cork towns. It was agreed that Major General Sean Hales and John L. would set out by boat from Dublin with a number of men and land at Bantry Bay. According to John L., when the plan was put into practice, they had no difficulty in landing and capturing the town. Local men joined them and by the time they got to Skibbereen, they had about 150 extra men. The numbers increased as they moved along; they took Rosscarbery, Clonakilty, Courtmacsherry. They then headed towards Kinsale and took the town as part of the overall strategy. At the same time, a massive invasion of Cork city was planned. Dalton set out by boat with a number of men, prepared to capture the city. Collins had engaged his sister, Mary Collins-Powell, to liaise between himself and Emmet Dalton in Cork. She organised a volunteer force to help her brother. Collins was prepared to allow his sister to take the risk required in a Civil War, because he was anxious for a speedy conclusion.[51]

Collins, preoccupied with military matters, had, meanwhile, left the political arena to Griffith, Cosgrave, O'Higgins and others. "We have shown our determination to uphold the people's rights," he wrote. "It is at this moment merely a question of time to complete the clearing of those people. We want to avoid any possible unnecessary destruction and loss of life."[52]

In the south, with strong key men, Collins's military tactics were bearing fruit. By 10 August, Dalton and his men were making steady progress in Cork, but were hampered due to a shortage of men; Dalton requested Collins to send 300 more[53] and when they were not coming Dalton pleaded, "I simply must get reinforcements immediately. I am at a standstill."[54]

Immediately Collins organised the transportation of reinforcements by boat and decided he would embark on an Army-inspection tour of the south, taking in Limerick and Kerry. If all went well, he would proceed to Cork.

Chapter 1

General Michael Collins, Commander-in-Chief of the Irish Army, was killed in an ambush by irregulars at Béal na mBláth , between Macroom and Bandon, on last night, (Tuesday). Towards the close of the engagement, which lasted close upon an hour, the Commander-in-Chief was wounded in the head.

This notice appeared in large print on the front page of *The Irish Times* and *The Irish Independent* on Wednesday, 23 August, 1922, at a period when Ireland was being torn apart by a bloody Civil War.

Michael Collins's body lay guarded by four soldiers in room 121 of Shanakiel Hospital in Cork city. The crown and poll of his head were encased in bandages. His fingers were entwined around a crucifix.

He was clad in the officer's uniform which he had worn for the first time just ten days previously, at the funeral of his friend and colleague, Arthur Griffith.[1] In a chair to the right, his greatcoat was casually thrown. An officer came into the room, went to the other side of the iron-framed bed, and placed on the locker a blood-streaked cap, also Collins's Sam Browne belt and detached holster.[2]

At this early hour a hushed stillness pervaded the room as the officer left. Three large candles burned at each side of the bed; shadows flickered behind the closed curtains. Soldiers stood in silence;[3] their task was to guard the body of a man who for the best part of six years had cheated death while he fought for the freedom of Ireland; a man who had indicated that he didn't want to die in his own county of Cork. Yet, on

Saturday, 19 August 1922, the day before his County Cork visit, he seemed to have had an intuition that the die was cast.

Outside, arrangements were being made for the removal of the body to St. Vincent's Hospital, Dublin. Later it would go to the City Hall for the lying-in-State. The main road to Dublin was impassable at various points: blocked as part of the Republican strategy; barricaded by fallen trees, trenches, and blown-up bridges. Consequently arrangements were being made for the removal of the cortege by the SS Classic which had arrived at Cork harbour from Fishguard earlier that day.

The Irish people now mourned the death of a hero, a leader and a man of principles: the laughing boy from Clonakilty, Co. Cork, who became a soldier, who helped to organise the Irish Republican Army into a fighting force, who cracked the British intelligence network in Ireland, who became a wanted man as the British Government placed a reward on his head, who was a negotiator and one of the signatories in the "Articles of Agreement for a Treaty between Great Britain and Ireland," who later became Chairman of the Provisional Government and Minister of Finance, who formed a War Council and became Commander-in-Chief of the Army during a bitter Civil War.

Dr. Leo Ahern, one of the doctors who carried out the medical examination following Michael Collins's admission to hospital, had certified him dead.

Yet, sixty-seven years later his death has not been officially registered.

Over twenty miles away the early morning sun shone over Béal na mBláth valley. The mist which had shrouded the ambuscade on the previous evening had lifted.

It was 6 a.m. West of Béal na mBláth, three Republicans, Jim Kearney, Timmy Sullivan and Tom Hales, were in Jim Murray's field beyond the dwelling house and farmyard. Jim Kearney, on the instructions of Tom Hales, had got a shovel from Jim Murray and was digging a hole beside a tree.

Earlier, Kearney, Sullivan and a local man had found an

officer's cap at the scene of the previous night's ambush. The cap, which had a large bullet hole to the right of the back stitching, was blood-stained and contained a quantity of human matter.

The men brought it to Tom Hales who was billeted in Murray's house. Hales took the cap. "This is human flesh, and must be buried," he said.

As the men now stood close to the oak tree, Hales, with the aid of a penknife, carefully levered off the front badge and diamond. "A souvenir of a friend," he said sadly, and put it in his back pocket. He handed the cap to Kearney, who had dug a hole approximately a foot and a half deep. Kearney paused momentarily. "The penknife!" he said, stretching out his hand to Hales. With the shovel resting against his body, he severed the front strap from the officer's cap and put it in his pocket, but didn't speak.

Having completed the burial, Hales blessed himself; his two companions did likewise. Hales hesitated with bowed head. He had memories of his former friendship with Collins. (Hales was one of the founder members of the West Cork Volunteers. With Collins presiding, Cork No.3 Brigade was formed at a meeting in Kilnadur, Dunmanway on 5 January, 1919 and Tom Hales was elected commandant. Tom Hales had been arrested by the British in June 1920, severely tortured and imprisoned in Pentonville jail. While Collins was in London during the Treaty negotiations, he visited Hales on a few occasions. After the signing of the Treaty by Collins and the other plenipotentaries in December 1921, Hales was released. Though his brother Sean Hales backed Collins in the implementation of the Treaty, Tom took the anti-Treaty side. Afterwards Collins said, "More than any man, I would have valued his support.")

As the men stood beside the buried cap, Tom Hales recalled his last conversation with Collins when Collins said, "Sure we're all Republicans."

Hales responded, "Whatever you do, settle the thing."

"I can't. There's no alternative," said Collins.

"I'd find an alternative," said Hales.

"What's the alternative?" Collins asked.

"Death!" said Hales. "I'd die first."

Hales told the men that morning, "Mick meant as much to me as any of my brothers, and I thought a lot of my brothers."[4] He was unaware that on the previous day, while he and his Republican comrades lay in wait for Collins's convoy, Collins had said to Emmet Dalton, his escort in the touring car, "It's too bad he is on the other side now. Because he is a damn good soldier," and added pensively, "I don't suppose I will be ambushed in my own county." It is ironic that on that day also, Sean Hales, Tom's brother, was the last soldier to whom Collins spoke before leaving Bandon for Béal na mBláth, less than an hour before he met his death.

The three men who paused beside the spot where Collins's cap was now buried were unaware that their action was going to become part of a mystery that would not be solved for over sixty years; nor could they have anticipated that the cap would be one of the principal pieces of evidence in establishing how Michael Collins was shot.

Kearney handed Collins's revolver, which the men had found on the ambush location, to Hales, and told him of the motorbike that the outrider had abandoned on the roadside.

Chapter 2

Michael Collins rose to prominence during the War of Independence when as Director of Intelligence and of Republican activities he earned the loyalty of his friends and evoked the enmity of his British opponents. Having played a vital part in the Treaty negotiations and put his signature to the Articles of Agreement, he was determined thereafter to uphold his decision.

As Chairman of the Provisional Government he struggled, along with his former comrades to re-unite the army in the twilight months that led to a Civil War. During this period, difficulties arose for him as he tried to reconcile the divergencies between the military and the political elements within the cabinet. The situation often led to a dualistic approach by Collins when on the one hand he tried to remain loyal to the Treaty, and on the other he co-operated with the anti-Treaty men, especially in matters regarding the north of Ireland.

By early July the anti-Treaty forces were in command in large areas of the country so the Provisional Government had to make a stand. Collins was thus willing to accept the challenge of his "appointment as Commander-in-Chief of the National Forces."[1]

On 12 July, temporarily relieved of his duties as Chairman of the Provisional Government and Minister of Finance (posts to which he intended returning when the war was over), he donned his military uniform and moved into quarters at Portobello Barracks.[2]

The prestige of soldering appealed to him: he had several photographs taken of himself in uniform and he liked the idea that "men should be ready for inspection by the

Commander-In-Chief. Every man who could be spared should be on parade."[3] He wrote memos suggesting how members of the National Army should present themselves.[4] Inefficiency disturbed him. Only a small proportion of the soldiers were men who had fought in the War of Independence. Some were young recruits while others were Irish soldiers who had fought in the British Army. Collins saw it as his responsibility to make them into a respectable "National Army."

Collins was a man who liked to joke provided the joke was not on him.[5] He was intolerant of the shortcomings of others; loyal to a certain point, but at that point he was prepared to bend the rules to suit a particular situation. He was an extremely sharp man at evaluating situations and people and a very methodical planner. These qualities became evident once he took over as "Supreme Commander" of the National Army. He coined the title "Irregulars" for the opposing forces (a label which was detested by them), insisted that newspaper reporting should substitute this title for the word "Republicans" and ordered that "descriptions of a military operation must not be published while the operation is still uncompleted."[6] (See also Appendix III.)

Tireless, he pushed himself to the limits. He had set himself a task of building up a true Irish state, one based on the culture which "showed itself" most strongly along the western seaboard. "South and West and Northwest", he wrote. "To those places the social side of anglicisation was never able very easily to penetrate … It is only in such places that one gets a glimpse of what Ireland may become again."[7]

Being convinced that there was only so much he or any leader could do, because "leaders are but individuals and individuals are imperfect, liable to error and weakness," he believed that the future rested in the people's hands. " The strength of the nation will be the strength of the spirit of the whole people."[8]

There were times when he seemed to have a premonition of death. He would become morose, express a fatalistic view to a friend, but would just as quickly snap back into joviality. It was as if he didn't want to ponder on the negative. In his new role, as Commander-in-Chief, he threw himself fully into the task. Michael Hayes, a colleague, said of him: "He had shown he could work with others and with Richard Mulcahy he had always found co-operation easy, though in some ways they were different types of men. They shared a capacity for hard work, determined character and a total devotion to duty."[9]

By the second week in August it was time for him to move into the country to review the military posts. But first he would meet members of the 2nd and 3rd Northern Divisions. At the meeting in the Officers' Mess, Portobello Barracks, "The Government and the Army was represented by Michael Collins," with Richard Mulcahy presiding, according to Thomas Kelly, a member of the 2nd Northern division who was present:

"The position of the six counties was examined fully and carefully. Many and varied views were expressed, some quite heatedly, but the only statement of importance was the final summation and decision of Michael Collins," who said, "with this Civil War on my hands, I cannot give you men the help I wish to give and mean to give. I now propose to call off hostilities in the North and to use the political arm against Craig so long as it is of use. If that fails the Treaty can go to Hell and we will all start again."[10]

By this time Collins believed that the anti-Treaty forces "were beaten as an open force." He was "definitely on the idea of having some arrangements that would save the faces of the anti-Treatyites and enable them to stop fighting."[11] With this in mind, he would take a trip to the country and talk to the men on location. So on Saturday, 12 August, he "left Portobello barracks at 4 a.m. exactly"[12] on an inspection tour. He would visit Kerry and cross the border into County Cork.

During his first official stop at Maryborough prison, his eye, sharpened by years of practising intelligence work, fell on the grey colour that went right to the top of the prison wall. This, he felt, would facilitate prisoners who were trying to escape. After he left "a strip at the top of the wall was whitewashed." It was no pleasure to him to find that prisoners had decided to engage in throwing utensils at him as he walked through the ground floor—these were his own people!

The convoy drove to Limerick and while Collins was there he sent a message to Mulcahy asking him to send "tenders, spare parts and some Lewis guns" immediately because the Army were "moving forward against hostile positions."[13] Also he said he "must know" what "communications with Cork city" were like.[14] Mulcahy confirmed that communication with Cork was "only by boat and wireless." He had wired Dalton to communicate with Collins, because Dalton had reported on 12 August that Cork was "entirely in his hands."[15] Following this good news, Collins moved on to army centres at Patrickswell, Adare, Rathkeale, Newcastlewest and Abbeyfeale. At each venue he noted various activities which required attention; "any orders given were given with instructions to report" to O'Duffy when orders were completed.[16]

When Collins visited Coolbunion House in Castleconnell he became extremely angry at the lax attitude of the men. Sentries were not on duty at the various entrances. "The actual approach to the entrance of the house was filthy in the extreme." In a long letter to O'Duffy after his return, he summed up the situation by saying, "The whole appearance of the men and surroundings were unbecoming of army men."[17]

During this journey, Collins and his men encountered a number of problems: the Lancia went on fire at Naas and only started with difficulty and the Crossley tender ran out of petrol near Roscrea. According to Collins's letter, "both the Tender and Lancia would have been left on the road were it not for a supply of aviation spirit, which was being taken at the request of the Air Service to Limerick." They had problems with a spare wheel, and during the journey in Kerry the armoured car supplied from Limerick got "ditched" "due to an incompetent driver." Being a man who disliked slovenliness, he wanted to know, "Who exactly was responsible for passing the fleet as fit in every way?" because, "in the whole journey nothing happened that could not have been avoided by care, attention and ordinary foresight."[18]

He had intended travelling from Kerry to Cork, but on reaching Tralee late that night he received news that Arthur Griffith had died. Though Griffith had been unwell for some time, his death came as a shock to Collins who maintained that, " he had sounder political judgement than any of us."[19]

Early the following morning, 13 August, Collins returned to Dublin for the funeral. This meant the postponement of the County Cork military barracks' inspection.

There was an air of confidence for Collins and the military men by this time. *The Irish Independent* reported on 16 August that "The National Army are advancing with no one to say them nay ... Of the thousands of irregulars who occupied Cork County a month ago there is no trace."[20] Regular supplies were now leaving Dublin for Cork by sea,[21] and Mallow, which was considered a gateway to Cork city, was now in the hands of the Government forces. "The war in its first stage may be considered to be over," *The Irish Independent* reported. "True that in Macroom a few irregulars still are to be found who may confound expectations by making some resistance."[22]

Meanwhile, aerial reconnaissance of the vast southern region was undertaken by Pilot Comdt. Russell and Capt. Stapelton.[23]

On Wednesday morning, 16 August, Collins telephoned Cosgrave[24] before calling on Sir John and Lady Hazel Lavery. He met members of the Provisional Government, and together they went to Arthur Griffith's funeral Mass at 10.30.am. This was followed by the processional march to Glasnevin cemetery.[25]

As he walked through the Dublin streets behind the coffin, he stoically bore the loss of his dear friend and counsellor. On the same morning Collins got word that Dunne and

O'Sullivan had been hanged (10 August) in Wandsworth prison, London, for the shooting of Sir Henry Wilson. O'Sullivan had written a letter to his mother in which he listed a number of people to whom he wished to be remembered; included in the list was the name of "Micky Collins." The same Collins had tried unsuccessfully to obtain a reprieve for the two men.

A bystander remarked on Collins's grim expression as he walked behind the coffin at the head of his Staff. "Ireland's problems hang heavily on his shoulders."[26]

In a graveside tribute to Arthur Griffith Collins said, "He always knew what Irish Nationality meant, just as Davis knew it. He never confused it with English Nationality. Some of our present day political leaders have done this under the guidance of English minds ... In memory of Arthur Griffith let us resolve now to give fresh play to the impulse of unity, to join together one and all in continuing his constructive work, in building up the country which he loved."[27]

Silently he moved back and stood, head bowed, beside the grave of his friend. His work was not yet concluded. His tour of inspection of southern counties had to be completed; with most of the major towns and cities in the hands of Government forces it looked to him as if the Civil War would soon be over. The slow processional march to Glasnevin carried a certain amount of strain. Relieved that that part was over, he sighed: "I hope nobody takes it into his head to die for another twelve months."[28]

That evening Collins went back to the barracks where he wrote a considerable number of letters.[29] At 8 o'clock he went to the Laverys' home where Lady Hazel hosted a pleasant evening meal. He was pleased to be with friends after the ordeal of the earlier part of the day. At 10.30 p.m. he left for Baldonnell to pick up "air service reports."[30]

On Thursday morning, 17 August, Collins received a letter from Eoin O'Duffy in Limerick stating that a Mr Hayes had brought a letter to O'Duffy requesting Commandant General Hannigan to issue to Dan Breen, "a safe conduct" pass to see Collins. O'Duffy told Hayes that the matter would be considered; he would not issue "a Safe Conduct to Dublin without first knowing" whether Collins "would receive Dan Breen or not." O'Duffy said, "I respectfully suggest that you refuse to see him."

In this letter O'Duffy explained how much territory was now held by the National forces. With Dalton in the Cork area and Prout in Waterford "with all three ... working in co-operation for a week which would bring us up to the 25th August, we might then be in a position to negotiate with advantage." Therefore he expressed his view of the "importance of holding fast," as it was his belief that "the Labour element and Red Flaggers are at the back of all moves towards 'Peace,' not for the sake of the country, but in their own interests ... This is why I suggest to you, not to see Breen or any of the others ... "[31]

Collins, who consistently liked to confide his ideas to paper, jotted down some notes: "It may be well to keep open some avenue or avenues to peace. Advantages of making a public offer giving them an opportunity of (a) going home without their arms. (b) Behaving decently in support of the administration, and in acceptance of the People's verdict we don't wish for any surrender of their principles ... "[32] These notes suggest that Collins did not want to close any door that might lead to peace.

Collins decided that he would resume his review of the forces in the south, see the situation for himself, and speak to the officers "on the ground." Immediately he sent a message to O'Duffy: "Am anxious to know progress towards Millstreet. Expect to see you linked up with Dalton everywhere within twenty four hours. See you about ten o'clock on Saturday."[33] His mind was made up. At this juncture he was not sure how far south he would go, but he was going south.

The following morning, Friday 18 August, he walked into the office of Joe McGrath, his intelligence officer and announced his intention of travelling south. McGrath protested, pointing out the danger. But Collins was determined that he was not "going to run from his own Corkmen," and told McGrath to get a convoy organised.

McGrath later wrote all his objections in red ink in a letter which he intended putting on Collins's desk. But on reflection he decided that when Collins gave an order he wanted it implemented without argument.

A wire message arrived from Dalton in Cork saying that "terms" had been communicated to him "by a Committee of prominent citizens of Cork." During a week's truce "facilities are to be afforded to the Republican military and political leaders to hold a meeting to discuss the making of peace."[34] Certain guidelines concerning arms, ammunitions and political prisoners, were listed.[35]

Collins responded by wire:

> Will you say by cypher who the prominent citizens responsible for the offer are? Have the Irregular Leaders, political and military agreed to the offer and is it made on their behalf?
> Government offer published in the Press 5th June, and conveyed to the People's Rights Association, Cork, stands... [36]

(See also Appendix 1V.)

In his habitual manner he wrote in his notebook, "Every constitutional way is open to them" (anti-Treaty forces) "to win the people to their side and we will meet them in every way if only they will obey the people's will and accept the authority of Government and of the people. That alone is our concern." Therefore "any further blood is on their shoulders. The onus placed unmistakably on their shoulders, the public must be kept aware of what we are upholding and of our willingness to avoid and prevent further loss."[37]

Next morning, Saturday 19 August 1922, Hazel Lavery telephoned Elizabeth, Countess of Fingall because a number of important people had been invited to dinner at Kilteragh House in Foxrock, residence of Sir Horace Plunkett. She asked her friend, "Do you think Sir Horace would like me to bring Michael Collins over to supper tonight?" The

Countess said she felt Horace would be delighted as George Bernard Shaw was also invited and both were "interested in the idea of meeting the rebel leader."[38]

That same morning in Portobello Barracks Michael Collins was not feeling well. As he sat down to breakfast beside Richard Mulcahy he was "writhing with pain from a cold all through his body; and yet he was facing his day's work for that Saturday, and facing his Sunday's journey."[39]

In his Portobello office while he attended to some preliminaries he received the telephone call from Lady Hazel Lavery. Shortly afterwards he left the barracks and went to his friends, the Leigh Doyles, in Greystones. With Kevin O'Higgins and others he had been a regular visitor to the Leigh Doyles' home. On this occasion he asked them "to take care of" his fiancée Kitty, who was staying at the Grand Hotel.

Recently he had had a picture taken of himself in uniform. He gave them a copy; he would sign it when he returned from Cork. Now he was in a hurry.[40]

Back in his office he dealt with a vast amount of correspondence. There were also last minute decisions regarding his next day's journey.

Throughout the day Collins wrote reports on the Engineering Services and ammunition and various allied items in connection with "Aerodrome—Air Communication."[41] During what was to be his last day at his desk in Portobello Barracks he also wrote a tremendous number of letters. Though not in his usual top form, he wrote letters to the Director of Munitions,[42] the Director of Purchases,[43] the Director of Publicity,[44] the Director of Recruiting,[45] and to each of the commands in central barracks throughout the country. He required "Strength return and Nominal roll of all ranks,"[46] to be compiled "up to and including Thursday 24th inst 12 o'clock midnight," and this should include "every officer and other rank ... even if only on duty there for a few hours."[47] As Commander-in-Chief Collins required full statistics of the men under his control in order "to co-ordinate activities," and also to supply the cabinet with details for the next meeting of the Dáil.

Later in the evening, having checked with Joe McGrath that everything was in order for the morning, he was ready to relax for a few hours with friends. According to Sir John Lavery, Hazel was anxious that Horace Plunkett and Collins should meet. She took him to the Countess's house "the same evening alone. I was a little anxious, but for some reason did not go."[48]

Michael Collins signed his name in Irish in the visitor's book at Kilteragh House. (This Irish version, Micheál O Coileáin, was his usual signature.) He was not feeling well that night and because he was quieter than usual he did not impress Countess Elizabeth: "not at all an eloquent man, and my recollection of the dinner is that it was very quiet, and almost dull."[49]

The writer, George Bernard Shaw, met him that night "for the first and last time." He said he was "very glad" he did. "I rejoice in his memory ... "[50]

The guests, who included W. T. Cosgrave, left early because, in the words of Sir John Lavery, "Michael Collins said he had to be in Cork next day. A car with an escort followed them." They went "for a drive in the mountains,"[51] and while returning to the Salthill Hotel where Lady Lavery was staying, they were ambushed; "a half a dozen shots were poured into the car." On their arrival at the hotel Sir John examined the car with an electric torch: "it seemed a miracle that no one was hurt, for there were six people in the car, sitting close together." Collins's slight illness caused him to make light of the ambush; he was complaining of a pain in his side and thought it might be "his appendix."

Sir John eventually persuaded him to accept his hot-water bottle. Collins, placing it under his tunic, smilingly said that "the pain was gone." With a "God bless you both, he jumped into his car...dashing off into the night." That was the last time Sir John and Lady Lavery saw Michael Collins alive.[52]

When he reached Portobello Barracks, he told a colleague Joe O'Reilly how badly he had been feeling. O'Reilly made a hot drink with oranges and took it to Collins in bed.

"God that's grand!" said Collins.

These words of gratitude encouraged O'Reilly who on impulse bent down to tuck him in for the night. Collins, not used to such personal touches, gathered his strength and shouted, "Go to hell and leave me alone!"[53]

Chapter 3

Michael Collins's last journey began on Sunday 20 August 1922.

At 5.15 a.m. the unpainted wooden door of his room in the annexe at Portobello Barracks was opened. The Commander-in-Chief of the Army of the Provisional Government, dressed in his uniform, boots and gaiters, carried his officer's cap in his left hand with his gun-hand swinging loosely as he went down the steps and across the grounds for his breakfast. A few weeks previously he would have tripped the steps lightly, but this morning he walked. The big man looked tired and drawn as he made his way across the grounds to the officers' dining room. Soldiers stood back and saluted as he passed.

Fionán Lynch, about to join him for breakfast, asked how he felt. "It's that damn cold!" Collins responded. As Lynch handed him a cup of tea, he remarked that he was feeling "lousy yesterday but wasn't quite as bad this morning." He had this "desperate pain" in his side the previous night but that was now gone.[1] A faint smile crossed his face when he said, "It must have been the oranges that did the job," as he related how Joe O'Reilly had brought him the hot orange drink in bed.

Now, he put his customary two spoons of sugar in his tea.[2] While stirring his tea, he began to tell Fionán Lynch about the near escape he had had the previous night returning from Horace Plunkett's dinner party. "The end can sometimes be so near," he remarked.

He ate just one slice of bread, finished breakfast and got up. He wanted a few words with Joe McGrath, Director of Intelligence, before he set out on his journey. He mounted the stairs and went into McGrath's room. "You're a fool to go!" McGrath told his superior officer. But, Collins was adamant, "Whatever happens to me, my own fellow countrymen won't kill me."

Walking beside Joe McGrath, he went down the cement steps, then put on his military greatcoat and went into the yard. The loud hum of the armoured car greeted him. Already the men who were to travel in the Crossley tender waited for the vehicle, Reg. number (01 8818), driven by Captain Conroy. The original driver delegated to this job, Private Lyons, had been sent to Wellington barracks[3] where another tender was at the ready in case tender 01-8818 was not "up to" the journey,[4] because Captain Conroy had said that it "was not pulling well" the previous day. Tender 01-8818 was now being serviced.

Lieutenant John Joseph Smith, a motor-cycle scout, had his bike engine running.

O'Reilly, who had given Collins the orange drink the previous night, woke suddenly, and on impulse rushed to the window. Collins was standing outside on the steps. "He wore a small green kit-bag over his back, his head was bent in gloomy meditation and, thinking himself unobserved, he let himself fall slack in the loneliness and silence of the summer morning."[5]

The distinctive sound of the Crossley tender driven by Captain Conroy startled Collins. He saluted and made his way towards the touring car. Joe Sweeney rushed out the barrack door and said to Collins that he had only just heard of his intention to travel south.

"Wait until things are more settled. You could get killed."

"No one is going to shoot me in my own country," Collins said.

Driver M.B Corry sat behind the steering wheel of the Leyland Thomas Straight-eight touring car and co-driver, M. Quinn, sat in the passenger's seat. Fionán Lynch jumped into the back. He would share the seat with Collins as far as Limerick Barracks where a few items needed his attention.

Collins, about to embark on his final journey through the

country, mounted the Leyland. He sat beside Fionán Lynch, and in his efficient manner, took out his spiral notebook and jotted down, "Started 15 minutes late—Valve-spring broken in Fiat."[6]

Lieutenant Smith, the motor-cycle scout-rider, led the convoy which set out from Portobello Barracks at 6.15. a.m. Next was the Crossley tender, driven by Captain Conroy, with a complement of twelve men including Sergeant Cooney, Captain Joe Dolan, and Captain Peter Conlon, and the man in command of the escort, Commandant Sean (Paddy) O'Connell. Among the men were two machine-gunners to operate the Lewis-gun.

Next in line was the Leyland Thomas Straight-eight touring car carrying Collins and Fionán Lynch.

Bringing up the rear of the convoy was the Rolls Royce Armoured Car, Reg. number ARR 2 and called *Slieve na mBan*, which was to play an important part in subsequent events. This was driven by Private Jim Wolfe, with co-driver Private Jimmy "Wiggy" Fortune. Seated in the back was Private Wally Coote, and Lieutenant Gough. Machine-gunner Private John (Jock) McPeak was in charge of the revolving-turret Vickers water-cooled gun.

It was late on Saturday afternoon when most of the crew were informed of their forthcoming journey. Jim Wolfe had been Sean Hales's driver during the early stages of the Civil War.[7] Jimmy McGowen, the usual driver of the *Slieve na mBan*, was sick, so Jim Wolfe was asked by Captain David Coates to take McGowen's place at the wheel.

Collins, having noted the problems with the tender, wrote in his personal notebook, "Is there a manifest of cars?"[8] He spoke to Fionán Lynch about the problems which he had encountered during his journey to Limerick and Kerry the previous week, when the convoy had had several mishaps and eventually they had to get a replacement tender. He was "annoyed" because the "difficulties which had arisen on that occasion could have been avoided," if due care had been taken.[9]

The convoy of soldiers and officers of the Provisional

Government's army with their Commander-in-Chief headed through the side streets of Dublin. Though it was Sunday morning, this complement of men couldn't risk going to Mass or Church Service. Church bells chimed in the early morning, as nuns in their convents and brothers of religious orders went to pray.

Through the outskirts of the city the convoy drove on its way towards the first stop at Portlaoise Barracks. Once out on the country road, Collins relaxed, according to his travelling companion, Fionán Lynch. "Both hands rested on his thighs," he talked to Lynch, saying that while he had grown accustomed to city life, "deep in his veins there was always this love for the country." Despite his heavy cold, he was in "reasonably good spirits," with occasional "bursts of high spirits." But it angered him when they "encountered destruction caused by Irregulars."[10]

The August sun and the sight of the open fields and bogs appeared to revitalise him. He told Lynch that he hoped he would be able to get to Cork city and further; his true wish was "to visit his old home place and his relatives and friends in West Cork."

As they headed into Portlaoise there were pony-traps of Sunday worshippers leaving the town. Sometimes those on foot stopped and looked after them; others paid no attention. In the open yard of Portlaoise Barracks Collins dismounted and went to the O/C's office where they discussed the condition of the army stationed there. The jail was over-crowded with prisoners. Collins said that some of them would shortly be transferred to Gormanstown camp which was in the process of being re-wired and made more secure in order to hold extra prisoners. (Provisions were also being made for Gormanstown camp to hold some prisoners from Kilmainham.)

Collins took a brief walk around the camp. Outside in the open yard he paused momentarily, took his note book and pencil from his top pocket and noted "Prisoners—for removal of say 200. Cipher to Dublin."[11]

After a further brief chat the two officers saluted and

parted. Collins got back into the Leyland and the convoy journeyed towards Roscrea.

It was after 9 a.m. when the convoy drove into Roscrea Barracks. After a brief inspection by Collins, some words with the O/C and with Tom Waters, Intelligence Officer, the full convoy sat down to breakfast.

Seated in the Leyland once more, Collins remarked to Lynch that he was feeling much better. There would be no further stops until they reached Limerick. This territory was in the hands of Government forces, so there were no road blocks or obstructions.

At Limerick military barracks the party were received by the G.O.C. Southern Command, General Eoin O'Duffy.[12] There was a private joke, a brief laugh as General O'Duffy remarked to his superior officer that it wasn't West-Cork bacon they would have for lunch, but the best Limerick bacon and Limerick cabbage.

After the meal Collins took out his memo book and jotted down a few items discussed during their conversation: "...to wire for two doctors," one for hygiene and the other for examination of recruits. "Two strong fellows" were to report to General O'Duffy the next day.[13]

On the way into Limerick, Collins had noticed that the bridge at Annacotty was down. He ordered that it should "be rendered safe for traffic" immediately.[14]

At 2.35 p.m. he drafted a letter to Mulcahy, to inform Diarmuid Hegarty that the new forms for the army "must include many more particulars, among them authorisation to pay dependents' money to some definite person."[15]

There were many items which he and O'Duffy had to discuss; he had wired O'Duffy on 15 August in connection with matters which he had noticed during his previous tour south towards Kerry before Griffith's death.

O'Duffy was now able to inform Collins that his orders had been carried out.[16] Collins believed the Civil War was almost over; he didn't want any rancour, he said. The two men discussed the suggestion that Lieutenant Colonel Frank Thornton should make contact with Dan Breen. Fr. Dick

McCarthy, a Limerick priest, was anxious to arrange a meeting between Breen and Collins and had suggested an old meeting place—Hickey's of Glenville.[17] Collins decided to consider the suggestion; he was always willing to keep his lines of communication open, but was in no rush, and certainly O'Duffy was against any compromise or meeting, at least for the present. Collins wasn't travelling on a peacemaking mission, according to Ernest Blythe, "though he was definitely on the idea of having some arrangement that would save the faces of the anti-Treatyites and enable them to stop fighting, but the onus was on them to stop."[18]

Michael Brennan, commander of troops in the Clare and east Limerick region, was in Limerick Barracks while the peace issue was being discussed. "It wasn't that he had any intention of offering a compromise, or giving any concessions," said Brennan who was convinced that Collins was not on a peace mission, but because "he was very attached to Cork men, like Lynch and Deasy, it was with reluctance he fought them."[19]

Frank Thornton left Limerick before Collins's own departure. As he travelled south of Clonmel that day, his convoy was ambushed at Ninemilehouse. Thornton was severely wounded and all the other members of his convoy were killed.

While in Limerick, Collins asked Tipperary soldier Jerry Ryan to send fifty of his best fighters to West Cork, because he was determined to end the conflict. (The Tipperary reinforcements were to travel by boat from Limerick to Bantry.)

At 4.05 p.m. he noted:

"Tell QMG [Quarter Master General] that an ambulance is required here and that it should be sent with the doctors who were asked for in my earlier wire." Also that "O'Duffy wants specially one hundred revolvers."[20] In addition he wanted to know when the Civic Guards would be ready to come to Limerick. "These must be regarded as members of the Army under the special conditions of their enlistment and are capable of being used for all duties."[21] He discussed with

O'Duffy the training of Civic Guards which was at that time being undertaken at the Curragh.[22] A division of these would be allotted to Limerick.[23]

Following a review of the prisoners Collins realised that there was much over-crowding in "conditions which endangered their health," also that "defence" was bad. He told Mulcahy in a wire that it was "essential" the "first removal" should be from Limerick where "there are four hundred and seventy" prisoners.[24]

After Collins had completed his business in Limerick, it was agreed that Eoin O'Duffy and an accompanying convoy would travel with the group to Mallow. At 5 p.m. the convoy left Limerick.[25] They drove out the dusty roads towards Kilmallock for a brief inspection. The clouds still hid the sun as they resumed their journey along the Limerick/Cork border and headed towards Charleville, then on to Buttevant. They arrived at Mallow shortly after 7.30 p.m.[26]

From here O'Duffy branched off, visited Kanturk, Millstreet and went on to Rathmore, Killarney "and other areas under his command." (He was ambushed on three occasions during this tour.)[27]

Collins spoke with Commandant Flood at the Mallow military post in the Royal Hotel and asked him to get word to Charleville in connection with "making good a passage over the Awbeg" river.[28] This he jotted down in his notebook—a reminder that when he got to Cork City he should see that "Engineering help" would be sent "to Mallow re Blackwater."[29]

The anti-Treaty forces, for their own protection, left roads mined, and damaged bridges as they evacuated areas. It angered Collins to find such destruction. The destruction of the Awbeg bridge meant that the Cork/Dublin railway line was out of action; it was for this reason that Collins's sister was unable to travel by train and pass on important information.

Archdeacon Corbett along with the Bishop of Cloyne, Dr. Roche, happened to be in the Hotel talking to Commandant Flood about the broken-down Mallow bridge when Collins arrived. The Archdeacon asked when the bridge would be repaired. "Give me a chance," Collins protested, and promised to have workmen there within a month.

"How is the struggle going?" the Archdeacon enquired. To this, he got the brief answer that things were going well enough and that Collins hoped for a speedy reconciliation. Then Collins wheeled around and walked away. "The poor man is in a hurry to meet his death," came the Archdeacon's prophetic remark. [30]

The main Cork/Mallow road was blocked by fallen trees and in addition, there was the fear that it would be mined. Therefore John O'Connell, a local man with knowledge of the by-roads, volunteered as an escort.

Continuing on the journey, the convoy jolted its way by the mountain route, an arduous task on the rudimentary road, especially with the cumbersome *Slieve na mBan*. In Monee, the convoy halted at Dan O'Keeffe's farmhouse to check the over-heated radiator of the Leyland and to replenish the radiators of the vehicles with water; this allowed some of the soldiers in the tender to take a breather. Shortly afterwards they resumed the journey and headed towards Whitechurch where a gathering had assembled at the cross-roads. The driver of the touring car became nervous and was on the point of pulling up when Collins shouted, "Drive on, you fool. Don't you see it is only the usual Sunday evening cross-roads dancing."

It was almost dark when the convoy headed through Blackpool and into Cork city. Passers-by were alerted as it stuttered down the South Mall in the stillness of the night. The military headquarters at the Imperial Hotel were well lit. And just as the personnel at the barracks along the way were taken by surprise, so was Emmet Dalton, Commander of the Cork region. Dalton knew that he was due a visit from Collins, but he wasn't sure of the date. He was just wording a wire in connection with peace moves; this he intended sending in the morning.

Collins stepped from the Leyland and strode into the Hotel. Seated side-by-side in the lobby he found two sentries with head bowed in sleep. Irritated at the spectacle, he seized them both, in dashing style banged their heads together and walked on.

News of Collins's arrival in Cork soon spread and shortly a cheering crowd gathered around the Hotel. Because Collins was a type of folk hero they wanted to catch a glimpse of him. Inside he met some of his old friends, and even a chance meeting with his sister Mary Collins-Powell somehow replenished his vigour. Mary Collins-Powell was about to leave the Imperial Hotel after having spent some time in conversation with Emmet Dalton when her brother walked in the door. The two had a brief chat and planned a further meeting for the morning. His nephew, Sean Collins-Powell, a member of the Provisional Government forces who had already fought in the War of Independence, drank a cup of tea with him and upon discovering that his uncle was taking a trip to the country the following day, asked if he could join, but was quickly told that they both had their own jobs. "You see after your own work, and I'll do mine," was Collins's response.

Emmet Dalton discussed the military position and also the peace moves. He was of the opinion that the National forces were in a stronger position than at any time previously. "I could not see any reason why we should compromise. This, also, was Collins's belief."[31]

Collins was consistently forthright in either praise or chastisement; on this occasion he complimented Dalton and his officers on their successful campaign. Since the capture of Cork on 12 August there didn't appear to be any military opposition. Anti-Treaty forces had fled to rural pockets—such as areas north of Newcestown and around Ballyvourney. On the Cork-Bandon road, they had felled trees and blown up the bridges at both Ballinhassig and Innishannon in accordance with the strategy of guerilla warfare, which was, as they saw it, their only hope of retaining control of certain areas.

It was now past midnight. Most of the men had gone to bed, some to quarters in the Victoria Hotel. Collins was feeling much better. Some of his old energy had returned and with Dalton, he made plans for the morning, and said that he looked forward with renewed optimism to an end to the strife. There was vigour in his step as he mounted the stairs of the Imperial Hotel and walked towards the bedroom which he was to share with Joe Dolan.

He plonked himself on the end of the bed, pulled off his boots and hurled them outside the door. "If you wake first, call me," he shouted across to Joe who had the sheet pulled half way up his face. Then there was a loud bang as Collins took a flying leap into bed.

Chapter 4

At five minutes to six in the morning he hurried down the stairs. Collins had decided that Monday 21 August 1922 was to be packed with activity. After breakfast he sat with Emmet Dalton at the mahogany table in the long room, planning the day's schedule.

The two men were friends since the War of Independence when Dalton had undertaken daring tasks. They had been in London together during the Treaty negotiations, and now they were helping one another to end hostilities. Dalton, a twenty year old, slim built, active man with British Army experience, was the anchor-man in Cork. Since he and fellow-officers and men had taken the city, it was discovered that there were matters of finance requiring immediate attention so that the wheels of the Provisional Government could get into full motion.

But first there had to be a tour of inspection of military posts in the city. It annoyed Collins that discipline was lax at one of the depots and he let his annoyance be known to the officer in charge. It wasn't, he said, because the city was in the hands of Government forces that they should allow disorder to creep into the force; as Commander-in-Chief he would see to it that the country would have a strong disciplined "National Army."[1]

He visited his sister, Mary Collins-Powell, and spent some time talking privately to her. "She had been in contact with him over the previous few weeks, mainly because she was organising a volunteer unit to assist my forces," said Emmet Dalton.

Among the subjects they discussed were the organisation of the new Civic Guard Force and the Customs and Excise service. Because Patrick Powell, Mary Collins-Powell's husband, was a Customs and Excise official, he had inside information about irregularities that were taking place: Republicans were diverting Customs and Excise funds that rightly should have gone to the Provisional Government and were using them for their own purposes. Later in the morning, Collins was able to act on this information when he called to the Customs and Excise offices in Cork.

At 9.30 am, Collins sent a wire to William Hogan at Portobello Barracks: "Ask Cosgrave wire at once, who used take charge of letting places like Moor Park, Kilworth, also representative Home Affairs, must be sent here regarding ordinary prisoners, courts, justices."[2] Here he appears in his ministerial rather than military role, trying to prevent anti-Treaty misappropriation of rental income, and concerned about the courts and the judicial system.

In order to expedite the Provisional Government's military campaign in Cork he sent a message to "tell Russell that Fermoy suitable for landing. Ask him if he could fly over West Cork area as follows: Macroom to Ballyvourney to Inchigeelagh, Bandon to Dunmanway." He was "most anxious to have these places reconnoitred."[3]

Collins and Dalton then went to meet the proprietor of the *Cork Examiner*, Tom Crosbie, at 10.30 a.m.[4] Collins wanted to discuss with him the general army position on publicity, also "the writing up of the situation" on the "People's Rights" viewpoint (a neutral group that worked for reconciliation) and "peace offers" which were being promoted.[5]

The anti-Treaty forces had blown up the printing works of the *Cork Examiner* before retreating from the city.[6] "They caused eighty thousand pounds worth of damage to property," according to Mr. Crosbie, because "since the beginning of August the *Cork Examiner* had taken a firm stand in favour of the Provisional Government."[7] Later that day Mr Crosbie would travel to London to try to buy printing presses.[8]

At 11 a.m. Collins and Dalton went to the Hibernian Bank and asked Mr. Pelly for "a brief statement"[9] regarding money which had possibly been deposited under the name of some Republicans.[10] They called to the Bank of Ireland at 11.15 a.m,[11] the Land Bank at 11.45 a.m,[12] then to various other banking institutions to try to recover £120,000 which the anti-Treatyites had obtained illegally from the Revenue Commissioners; it was mainly Excise duties belonging to the Customs and Excise offices in Cork. The anti-Treatyites had obtained this money by capturing the official collector and under threat of death they had made him sign the cheques which the banks honoured.[13]

A few days before this Desmond Fitzgerald in the Ministry of Economic Affairs had sent a report to "The Commander In Chief," and to "The Acting Chairman," which explained that "Banks in Cork city are keeping currency as low as possible … Cheques are being received at the Bank of Ireland noticeable to Excise and Customs and endorsed by Connell in which originally my 231 Customs & Excise is credited."

Desmond Fitzgerald noted: "The Irregulars have opened a No. 2 account (Customs & Excise account) in the same Bank authorising a rebel named Peter Ryan-Hervey to sign cheques to that account."[14]

Each bank that Collins and Dalton went into, they demanded that the manager should close the doors. They ordered the disclosure of "the names of the big business people who were acting as 'covers' for the Irregulars. We told them we would not allow the banks to re-open unless they revealed the full information. In this way, we got ninety per cent of the money back," said Dalton. They also got a tip-off about a certain church. "When we went there, the priest, after some persuasion, opened the tabernacle, where we found £3,000, which was being kept by the priest for the Irregulars." [15]

It was past 12 noon when they returned to the Imperial headquarters, where after a quick lunch, Collins with the convoy set out to review the military situation in Cobh. News of Collins's arrival in Cork had already travelled. Republicans in the Cobh district, anticipating that he might travel along the main road, had mined it at the outskirts of the town. However, fortune was on Collins's side on this occasion as the mine failed to explode.

After an inspection of the Cobh military post, the convoy returned to Cork city.

Though Collins loved the prestige of soldiering and the status of reviewing military positions, he expected to return to his duties as Minister of Finance as soon as normality in the military position was restored. He had been interested in figures ever since he passed the British Civil Service examination and worked as a youth in the London Savings Bank.

Meanwhile, he wanted to inform the Acting Minister of Finance about the banking transactions in Cork, so at 3.30 p.m. he wrote to Mr. Cosgrave:

(1) The Bank position here is slightly obscure. It will require a full investigation and combined with that investigation there must be our examination of the Customs & Excise position—all monies paid in and out must come under this. We shall require three first class independent men. Unfortunately Brennan[16] has gone to London.

(2) It would be very desirable to make an examination of the destination of certain drafts on the London County, Westminister & Paris, London. Childers (Mr and Mrs) kept and keep an account or several accounts at the Holborn (I think) Branch of this Bank. I am sure the Bank will give details of any recent transactions.

(3) I wired today re Moor Park & Kilworth—see Hogan and let him send down whatever man was dealing with this matter. It is urgent and we must collect back rent even though it may have already been paid to the Irregulars.

    The people here want no compromise with the Irregulars.

(4) It is wise to postpone the Dáil meeting as already suggested.

(5) You might get before your mind's eye three persons under Part 1, but don't announce anything until I return. [Bank position]

(6) It would be a good thing to get Civic Guards both
    here and in Limerick. Civil adminstration urgent
    everywhere in the South. The people are splendid.[17]

Collins was not seeking any "compromise" with the Republicans at this stage. According to Emmet Dalton: "Clearly
any hope which he had of settling the Civil War would not be
done at the expense of abandoning the Treaty." [18]

As telecommunications were extremely bad, Collins asked
that Frank Dalton should be assigned to the Cork P.O. with a
group of men while repair work was being carried out, in
order to protect the work from sabotage by anti-Treatyites.[19]

Collins had come to realise that the country was for the
most part in the hands of Provisional Government forces. His
desire to postpone the first session of the new Dáil indicates
that he was hardening in his attitude and wanted to finish the
fight. This was the impression that Dalton gathered from their
conversation. "If there was any negotiating to be done, it
would be from a position of strength. Collins didn't like to
see the split which had arisen in the Volunteer force. And like
all of us he had hoped for peace."[20]

It was almost 4 p.m. when the convoy assembled for the
journey to Macroom. Collins constantly tried to squeeze as
much as possible into every day. "I felt he wanted to do so
much in such a short time," said Dalton, who arranged that
the Dublin Liz armoured car would replace the *Slieve na
mBan* for this journey. (The *Slieve na mBan* was being
serviced at Johnson & Perrotts for its tour through West Cork
the following day).

The Macroom army post commanded by Peadar Conlon
informed Collins of constant attacks from some anti-Treaty
forces. In order to withstand the attacks, Conlon requested a
machine gun and some ammunition, which Collins promised
to have delivered early the following morning; he intended
spending the next day on an inspection tour of the full
command area in West Cork.

He was disturbed about a prisoner who had been taken in
by Lieutenant Coppinger and who had died; he queried the

circumstances and asked for a report. When Collins had completed his business in Macroom, the convoy returned to Cork.

Back in Cork, Collins and Dalton went immediately to a priest's residence in the hope of collecting further money held in safe keeping for the opposing forces. "Our information was correct," said Dalton. "When we told him [the priest] what we knew, he parted with a small box containing a large sum of money."[21]

Commandant Frank O'Friel, who had come down from Shanakiel hospital, was in the Imperial Hotel when the convoy returned from Macroom. Collins queried him about the wounded National soldiers, and asked for the names of those in hospital.

Word had come in, O'Friel said, that a Patrick Corcoran had died in the South Infirmary at 4 a.m. and that a Michael Collins had been fatally wounded when he rushed a machine-gun post at Rochestown. Collins said that this man was his cousin. Before going to bed that night, he wrote in his note book: "Michael Collins shot dead." Within twenty-four hours those ominous words would fit the man who wrote them.

Chapter 5

While Collins headed southwards on Sunday 20 August, 1922, de Valera was also moving in that direction.

Some days previously, de Valera was in Kilpeadar, near Ballincollig and had written in his diary: "Any chance of winning? If there was any chance, duty to hold on to secure it. If none, duty to try to get the men to quit—for the present. The people must be won to the cause before any successful fighting can be done. The men dead and gloomy—just holding on. How long will it last?"[1]

He had come into the Gougane Barra area on Saturday. The American writer, Peter Golden, found him in the neat whitewashed kitchen of James O'Leary. The house was tucked between the hills in the townland of Gurtafludaig, near Ballingeary.[2] The family were saying the Rosary in Irish when Golden entered the kitchen. De Valera was kneeling against the back of a súgán chair with his face buried in his hands. When the prayers ended de Valera rose and greeted the visitor, who got the impression that he was "heartsick and distraught at the terrible things which had come to the nation and its people."[3] Yet he discovered that de Valera hadn't a word of bitterness against those who opposed him. "Not even against those who certainly have not spared him." And though he spoke of the pioneering work for Ireland done by the late Arthur Griffith, he was "fearful that the next step will be a military dictatorship set up by Mick Collins, taking his orders from England."[4]

At this point in the war anti-Treaty military operations were outside de Valera's influence; these rested in the hands of the Army Executive, with Liam Lynch as Chief of Staff. Lynch had no intention of compromise, "We have declared for an Irish Republic and will not live under any other law," was his comment to his brother.[5] De Valera had met Lynch in Whitechurch. Lynch deluded de Valera by telling him to "see Liam Deasy" even though he felt at this stage that Deasy would be as adamant as himself. Meanwhile he sent a dispatch to Deasy, GOC of the First Southern Division in which he said, "Dev passing through your area talking of peace. Give him no encouragement."[6]

De Valera was hoping to locate Deasy, but because of the National Army's seaborne landings off the Cork and Kerry coasts, the principal strongholds of the anti-Treaty forces had been eroded. On 12 August, anti-Treaty forces abandoned Cork when pro-Treaty forces were making inroads through the city, thus avoiding civilian tragedies. They withdrew to secluded regions to the west of the city. Broken into units without any definite policy they were operating largely on the initiative of individual commanders during the week which followed. Republican leaders felt that the time had come for some cohesive plan.

Fighting in the field as a regular army had failed; guerilla tactics of the previous years were not operative because personnel, hide-outs, and movement-style were often known to local pro-Treaty troops. In addition, there were no established lines of communication between units and between these and the Executive headquarters. Consequently, when officers of Cork No.1 Brigade met in Ballyvourney on Sunday morning 20 August, Liam Deasy GOC was unaware of such a meeting until the following evening when he was informed by de Valera, who had been present.

Before the officers' meeting in James O'Leary's house, word had reached them from the Limerick area that Michael Collins was travelling south on a tour of inspection of Provisional Government forces. The men in Ballingeary felt that because of his interrupted tour of Kerry (interrupted to attend Arthur Griffith's funeral) Collins's convoy might this time travel along the Millstreet/Macroom route. And because so many important officers from the First Brigade were concentrated in the one area, it would be necessary to set up road blocks to avoid a surprise attack. The fact that it was an enemy contingent would of itself mean that it should be ambushed.

So roads into Ballyvourney and Ballingeary were blocked on that Sunday. Bill Powell waited in ambush position all day in charge of some men on the Carriganima/Millstreet road, while another section scouted on the Cloundroichead direction. Other roads were also being observed and mines were laid on the roads leading to James O'Leary's house. The main aim of the senior officers' meeting (chaired by Dan "Sando" O' Donovan O/C Cork No 1 Brigade) was to decide future policy. It emerged that though de Valera (who was present) talked of peace, the others wondered was there any way of fighting it out. "The men who were present were not for peace for the sake of it. It was hard, rough going, we debated everything thoroughly," said Sando. Finally, it was conceded that if Liam Deasy, G.O.C. (First Division anti-Treaty) agreed, he should put out some peace feelers. Then any new situation could be debated. De Valera informed the men that he was trying to locate Deasy.

During the meeting[7] Michael Murphy, Divisional Officer, and Sando O' Donovan (both described by Pake Sheehan as extreme Republicans) spoke about Collins.[8] The information received was that he was on his way southwards, with Cork on the itinerary. De Valera was told that if the convoy entered any hostile area where Republicans were based the convoy would be ambushed. When the idea was expressed that Collins "may not leave Cork alive" de Valera expressed regret as he felt it would be easier to negotiate with Collins than with other members of the Provisional Government or the Army.[9]

On Monday morning, 21 August, de Valera, fresh after his night's sleep in O'Leary's, set out once more to locate Deasy. Erskine Childers and Riobárd Lankford were known to be producing *An Phoblacht*, the anti-Treaty paper, on a hand-press in the home of Richard Woods at Moneygave, near Enniskeane.[10] It was decided to escort de Valera to this house where at least he would get an indication as to Deasy's whereabouts.

De Valera was taken by Paddy O'Sullivan in a pony-trap and reached Moneygave by mid-afternoon. Here Sean Hyde, publicity officer for the Republicans, had joined Childers and the brothers Riobárd and Joe Lankford. Later that evening Liam Deasy arrived. "They all gathered in the parlour and remained talking for the rest of the evening," said Maggie Sheehan, who was employed by the Woods family. "We brought in a few large pots of tea, eatables and the ware on trays. The men asked not to be disturbed, they said they would manage for themselves. When they wanted more tea, they came out to have the tea pots refilled."[11]

Riobárd Lankford said they discussed many issues including "the railroading of the Staters into our territory. Dev. was a good listener. We knew, of course, we were being beaten at the time, but we somehow hoped our luck would turn. Though we talked and talked, Deasy said that at the meeting the next day, when we would have officers from several regions, we could come to some positive decision."[12]

Earlier that morning, Liam Deasy had gone to his parents' home at Kilmacsimon and then to Sullivan's of Gurranreagh, the house that had been used as headquarters during the War of Independence. Deasy intended setting up temporary headquarters for the Division at Sullivan's and had notified Liam Lynch. Consequently among the many dispatches waiting for Deasy at Sullivan's was one from Liam Lynch informing him that de Valera had been with him, and was even then on his way to see him, and in Deasy's own words: "I was on no account to give him any encouragement as his suggestions and arguments were unacceptable to Lynch."[13]

Deasy soon discovered that Joe Sullivan, senior, was pro-Treaty and spoke with hostility about de Valera whom he called "the long fellow". It was made quite clear to Deasy that though he was personally welcome, he could forget about his intention of reinstating headquarters in the house for the anti-Treaty side.

Former billets had to be examined, intelligence work needed reorganisation, people's reaction in areas frequented by Republicans had to be studied, so that the anti-Treatyites could have shelter in safety and be sure of food; these were all matters which Deasy noted for the following day's meeting.

Because of the warning dispatch received from Lynch, Deasy wasn't completely taken by surprise when he saw de Valera in Moneygave; nor was he surprised at his suggestion of peace offers. "De Valera's principal argument was that we had made our protest in arms and appeared to be incapable of military success; the most honourable course for us would be to withdraw. I told him that we had at least a thousand armed men in the First Southern Division, and from my knowledge, most were prepared to fight on, and would not, therefore, agree to an unconditional surrender."[14] The war situation was discussed by the men until far into the night so that it was long past midnight when de Valera settled down for his sleep on "the settle in the parlour behind the door." Maggie Sheehan took a quilt from "the master's bed for the settle."[15]

Outside, Ned Galvin remained on scout duty throughout the night, in front of the house. (The Woods family were friends of Erskine Childers and their house was "a safe house" and headquarters for Republicans during the Civil War. From research it has emerged that de Valera did not stay in Sullivan's at Gurranreigh on this occasion, nor was their house headquarters for the Republicans during the Civil War, as has been stated in other writings.)

The following day, future policy was to be discussed further at an important meeting, which was convened for Bill Murray's house at Béal na mBláth. Deasy was glad that de Valera would be present to give his viewpoint.[16]

Chapter 6

Joe Dolan was startled by an early morning shout from Michael Collins on 22 August 1922. He jumped out of bed immediately. Collins was looking out the window. Cork city was silent in the sultry August morning. This Tuesday, the twenty-second of the month, was the beginning of the last day of Michael Collins's life.

The bell on Holy Trinity Church nearby was sounding the hour. At 6 a.m. Collins crossed himself and paused for a moment in prayer. Not a man to waste time dressing himself, he was, within seconds, down the stairs and into breakfast, which he ate hastily. He put on his officer's cap before tripping down the few steps to the footpath.

He saw the trim figure of Emmet Dalton, his travelling companion and body guard for the day. Dalton was pacing to and fro on the pavement. John O'Connell, who two days previously had acted as a guide on the route between Mallow and Cork, was no longer needed but had requested to remain with the group in order to tour West Cork. He was in the Crossley tender when Dalton emerged from the Imperial Hotel "as the hall clock read ten minutes past six." The convoy vehicles had left Johnson & Perrott's where they had been garaged, and had arrived outside the hotel at six o'clock. Lieutenant Smith the motorcycle scout was followed by the open Crossley tender with a complement of two officers, two machine gunners with a Lewis gun and eight rifle men; after this was the Leyland Thomas touring car in which Collins and Dalton would sit behind the two drivers, Corry and Quinn. Bringing up the rear was the *Slieve na mBan* armoured car driven by Jim Wolfe, with the crew men, and machine-gunner Jock McPeak.

Dalton saluted Collins, with the automatic gesture of a soldier—a formal display between two friends. They spoke briefly while Collins fingered the note book in his top pocket. Before mounting the Leyland, with poised pencil he glanced at the time, then jotted down: "Left at 6.15 a.m—Macroom, Bandon, Clonakilty, Rosscarbery, Skibbereen."[1]

While most of Cork city slept, the convoy broke the silence as it drove out along the Western Road and headed towards Ballincollig. Here they encountered what Dalton described as "an extraordinary amount of bridge destruction and road obstruction." Though they had travelled this route the previous day without much difficulty "it seemed as if the Irregulars had come and set up road-blocks overnight."[2]

Retreating from the city during the previous days, the Republicans had succeeded in making the main road to Bandon impassable by blowing up the bridges outside Ballinhassig and Innishannon. Dalton believed that the obstruction of the Ballincollig road was an afterthought; what he did not know was that Republicans travelling to the meeting at Béal na mBláth from the Ballincollig district were aware that a sudden swoop could leave many of their units leaderless—it was for this reason that Seán Hyde and a number of Republicans took the precaution of setting up road blocks. These blockages forced Collins's convoy to make a detour through by-roads in the Ballincollig area. They arrived in Macroom some time between seven thirty and a quarter to eight. The Lewis gun promised to Captain Conlon the previous evening was handed over. Collins, who had carried out an inspection in Macroom the previous day, didn't delay. He was anxious to proceed in the West Cork direction as quickly as possible.

Because he knew the road from Macroom to Bandon was blocked, Conlon suggested that Timmy Kelleher, who hadn't taken part in either the War of Independence or the Civil War, and who was employed as a driver for Williams Hotel, would be most suitable as a guide. Kelleher constantly took cattle buyers to all the fairs in the district, and was familiar with the area.

A soldier was sent to get Kelleher. Having been out late the previous night, he was still in bed, but was immediately awakened by the loud knock on the door. Once dressed he was informed by the soldier, who stood waiting, that he was to accompany a convoy as far as Bandon.

When Kelleher arrived at the Castle barracks he was informed that Collins was the principal passenger. This made him apprehensive. Shortly they were on the road. With Kelleher seated in the front of the Crossley tender, the convoy headed in the Crookstown direction. "I knew all the roads and was aware that two of the bridges on this line were broken, so we took the Dooniskey-Cross route," says Kelleher. They took a right turn at Dooniskey Stores and drove through the townland of Ballymichael. At the foot of the hill opposite O'Mahony's the Leyland stalled, forcing its occupants to alight.[3] At this stage, the Leyland showed the first signs of trouble, which according to Jim Wolfe, was due to dirty petrol. The petrol tins had been refilled without being emptied and had thus accumulated sediment since the beginning of their long journey from Dublin. (See Map 1.)

Some of the soldiers from the tender jumped out to assist, and when one soldier suggested to his Commander-in-Chief that he would take his place, Collins would have none of it, but pushed the car with the others to the top of the hill and down the small incline, where it restarted.

Seated once more, Collins joked about pushing "the old donkey" as the procession of vehicles proceeded towards Kilmurray. The convoy was again brought to a halt by a herd of cows driven by a farmer called Jerh. Murphy. Collins was in the heart of Republican territory but wasn't aware of it. Nor was any of the convoy members very alert to the danger. But Kelleher, the guide, suddenly became very aware of their vulnerability. He remarked to Conroy, the driver of the tender, as they headed into Kilmurray Cross where some men were assembled: "They're all Republicans over there. It looks as if there's an early morning gathering."

From Killmurray, it was on to Béal na mBláth Cross where the driver of the tender halted to check that the remainder of the convoy was following. The dispatch motorcycle rider also pulled up; he kept in touch with Kelleher who signalled directions to him. "When we stopped at the cross we were directly opposite Long's pub; in the upper right hand window facing us, there was a man looking straight at us—it could have been anybody. It was at that moment I became really aware that we were in Republican territory, and that no doubt our passing would be discussed. This thought flashed briefly through my mind, as the motorcyclist waited across the road for my signal."[4]

Realising that the remainder of the convoy was proceeding slowly but in sight behind, Kelleher signalled a right turn to Smith and so they headed in a direct line towards Bandon.

However, when the touring car reached the crossroads (it had been some distance behind), Quinn, the driver, discovered that there were four roads radiating from this point; he had lost sight of the vehicles in front, and as any of his passengers weren't exactly sure which of the roads to the right the leading vehicles had taken, he drove across to where a man stood and asked him the best road to Bandon.

Denny "The Dane" Long[5] was standing at the crossroads near the pub. He was a Republican scout armed with a rifle. He had been posted as a sentry at the crossroads because of the large number of Republican leaders who were gathered in the area for that day's meeting in Béal na mBláth. When he saw the motor cycle and tender passing he went into Long's public house which was at the corner and put his rifle behind the door. He saw the touring car approach and when it halted he felt safe enough because he hadn't a rifle. Instantly, he recognised Collins. Realising the dynamite situation which confronted him—at any minute armed Republicans could step out from the nearby pub or emerge from any of the roads—he quickly sent the "intruders" on their way. "The other lorry is gone straight ahead, and take the second cross to the right in the Newcestown direction," he said.

But what Long didn't know was that further on, Kelleher had directed Smith to take the straight road to Bandon, and not a right at the cross.

When Kelleher discovered that the convoy wasn't following, he immediately sensed what had happened, so the motor cyclist and tender made an about turn at a gap in a field and headed towards Newcestown where they found the vehicles parked outside the Church. Collins was reading the inscription over the door when Smith on his motor-cycle, followed by the tender, arrived. Collins raised his hand and returned to the touring car.[6]

As the convoy wound its way beside Curraclough and down Convent Hill towards Bandon, the August sun, hidden by the clouds since early morning, began to emerge. Their first stop was the Devonshire Arms Hotel, barrack-quarters of the pro-Treaty forces.

Bandon had been captured by pro-Treaty forces some days after Cork was taken. Collins regarded the town as the gateway to West Cork and only heard of the victory on the Saturday as he planned the Cork trip. The newspapers reported, "with the capture of Bandon the last of the Irregular strongholds has fallen but that does not mean that the last has been heard of the Irregulars." When the troops marched into the town on "Saturday evening the resistance offered was very weak."[7] Collins had received the news with satisfaction.

Bandon had been a stronghold of British imperialism since its foundation.[8] It was a garrison town and as such played a strong part in the upholding of British rule during the War of Independence. One of the most dreaded forces of British crown, the Essex regiment, which was stationed in Bandon, was involved in many bloody conflicts with Barry's Third West Cork Flying Column. Following the evacuation of the Bandon barracks after the signing of the Treaty, the Republican forces had been in command of the town. The Provisional Government was now in possession of the large military barracks in the square as well as both the Devonshire Arms quarters and Lee's Hotel.

This stop-over in Bandon was brief as Collins was anxious to continue his journey westwards. He spoke with Lieutenant Liam Daly, headquarters' officer and said that on his return call in the evening he would have a more detailed discussion with officers in the regional headquarters at Lee's Hotel. (Now the Munster Arms Hotel).

Breaking from protocol in typical fashion Collins cheerfully spoke to a former neighbour, Jack Sheehy. (Sheehy and Collins were born and reared in the same farmyard at Sam's Cross.) Collins put his revolver on the table, greeted Sheehy and took Sheehy's eight-year old daughter, Mary, on his lap. Their brief conversation ended with a warm handshake—the last Sheehy would get from the man who used to answer Mass and play hurley with him as a boy.

Tim Kelleher, who had been booked to take a passenger to Cobh in the afternoon, reminded Collins that he should get back to Macroom. Collins thanked Kelleher, and scribbled a note to hand to a taxi driver with a request to take him back to Macroom, and to collect the fee for the trip from barrack-headquarters in Bandon. As Collins held out the note, Kelleher asked, "How will you find your way back, Mr. Collins?" Instantly, Smith, the motor-cyclist, interrupted, "I know the way back now." To which Collins responded, "Good man!", shook hands with Kelleher and thanked him once more before stepping on to the Leyland.[9]

As the convoy crunched the stony road from Bandon towards Clonakilty, Collins discussed with Dalton the many ambushes that had been fought in the area. Since 1916, the people in the West Cork region had lived with uncertainty. There was hardly a home that hadn't been affected by the harsh and constant reality that the Irish people were fighting for freedom from British rule. Families who mourned the death of a friend or a loved one, killed either in an ambush or murdered in a Black and Tan reprisal, were united in their fight for independence. But since the signing of the 1921 Treaty and the outbreak of the Civil War, disharmony reigned in many homes. Local people were torn in their loyalties. If Michael Collins had not been involved in the negotiations and subsequent Treaty his friends and neighbours in West Cork have maintained that most, if not all, of the region would have decided to take the Republican side. As it was, only a minority had followed him, men who were in school with him, or men like Seán Hales and Ned Barrett who were in Frongoch jail with him.

But now on this August morning Collins and his men were travelling through this area recently recaptured by the troops of the Provisional Government, while some key Republicans were heading across fields to a meeting at Béal na mBláth.

Chapter 7

Tuesday 22 August 1922 was an important day for the Republicans. Officers from the five Battalions and some divisional officers under Liam Deasy GOC First Southern Division had been called to attend a meeting in order to assess the military situation and determine future policy. Since the previous evening, some of the men had been billeted in houses around Béal na mBláth as the meeting was to be held in Bill Murray's farmhouse, which was situated in an incline behind Long's public house, near where Collins's convoy had passed earlier. (See Map 3)

After breakfast, Liam Deasy, Sean Hyde, Jim Flynn and de Valera travelled in a pony and trap from Moneygave (approximately 3 miles) to Béal na mBláth, and arrived around 9.30 a.m. (Deasy had arranged that after the meeting, Dinny Crowley would accompany de Valera in the Glanworth direction to meet Liam Lynch.) When they got out of the trap at Béal na mBláth cross, they were immediately approached by Dinny "The Dane," who had been on scout duty since daybreak, having taken over from the night-watch. He told them that a "Free State armed convoy consisting of a motor cyclist, a lorry of troops, a touring car and an armoured car had passed earlier in the morning, and had stopped to enquire the way to Bandon." Dinny was "most helpful and sent them via Newcestown, knowing that road wasn't blocked." He was only too anxious to get them on their way because of the number of Republican Officers who were billeted nearby.[1]

Long told the men that he recognised Michael Collins seated in the back of the touring car.

"So he's on his way to West Cork!" was Deasy's initial

3. The people here want no compromise with the irregulars

4. It is wise to postpone the Dáil meeting as already suggested.

5. You might get before you minds & three persons under par 1, but don't announce anything until I return

6. It would be a big thing to get Civic Guards both here and in LIMERICK Civil Administration urged everywhere with South The people are Splendid.

Miceál O Coileain
21/8/22

Page from Collins's note book, written the day before he was shot

Collins in 1917

Kitty Kiernan, Collins's fianceé

John (Jock) McPeak, gunner of the
Slieve na mBan

Seán Hales

Collins greeted by friends

Tom Hales participant in Béal na
mBláth ambush

Tom Kelleher, participant in Béal
na mBláth ambush

Bill Powell, (standing), participant
in Béal na mBláth ambush

Jim Kearney, participant in the
Béal na mBláth ambush

Last photograph of Collins, taken outside Lee's
Hotel in Bandon on 22 August 1922. He and
Dalton are in the back of the touring car, Collins
on the left.

Oliver St. John Gogarty's death-mask of Collins

reaction. "Then he'll be coming back this way." Deasy knew that this was the only unblocked road to Cork because both the direct Bandon/Cork road and the "upper" Bandon road via Crossbarry had been rendered impassable; such strategy was necessary because of the many important officers and general staff of the Republicans who had been assembling in the area since the previous night. In response to this information, de Valera asked Deasy what he thought was likely to happen. Deasy said that there were a number of men billeted in the area who had been forced to retreat from Limerick, Kilmallock and Buttevant. "Some were involved in the Cork withdrawal, and because of this they are in a hostile frame of mind." Deasy further explained to de Valera that the area was predominantly Republican and that they would consider the entering of enemy forces as an intrusion. "In five company areas along this Bandon route, not one active volunteer joined the Free State Army. It seems like a challenge that they can't refuse to meet. It's most likely we'll prepare for an ambush."[2]

De Valera expressed sorrow on hearing this; his aspiration for peace was shattered. He had hoped after the Ballingeary meeting and subsequent discussion with Deasy, and the culminating meeting at Béal na mBláth, to have an overall view of the Republican mentality for the First Dáil meeting which he expected to attend.[3]

Disillusionment was evident on de Valera's face as he walked up the incline from the cross towards Murrays' house with a few men. Deasy had stepped into Long's public house at the crossroads to meet some of the officers who had spent the night there.

Bill Powell was at the top of the incline near the entrance to Murrays' when he saw de Valera approaching, so he waited. Powell mentioned that Michael Collins had gone past. "I can still picture him [Dev] looking out across the valley, no smile, stern as always, and all he said was, 'A pity! Pity I didn't meet him!' He turned, and we both walked silently along the rough stone of the yard and into Bill Murray's kitchen." Bill Powell was sorry the two men did not

73

meet, "If Collins had been later, or Dev. had been earlier, history could be so different. I'm pretty sure, that even though they were on opposite sides in a Civil War, they would have a few civil words in West Cork."[4]

The men who had already gathered in Bill Murray's kitchen were talking about Collins when de Valera walked in. Some who hadn't known de Valera was in the area were surprised to see him. Liam Deasy and other officers entered. According to Bill Powell, "There was no great debate, the question was, should an ambush be prepared or not? There was disagreement about this. Tom Hales was cool and thoughtful," said Bill Powell. He suggested that on balance they shouldn't ambush the returning convoy. (He had been very close to Collins.) However, when all views were expressed, it was finally decided that the convoy was part of an enemy force encroaching on territory which the Republicans still held and that therefore it should be ambushed.[5]

The agenda for the planned meeting was postponed. And de Valera, obviously sensing the mood of the men, left before full orders had been given to take up ambush positions. With his aide, Jimmy Flynn, he took the Cloughduv and minor roads (by-passing Cork city) and on to Mourne Abbey near Mallow.

The men who had assembled at Béal na mBláth were not a column, but officers who were trained in guerilla warfare and who had gathered to hold an important staff meeting. Seeing the opportunity of overpowering an enemy convoy on its return journey they decided to take up the challenge and ambush it.[6]

The area chosen was south of Béal na mBláth crossroads, an ideal ambush position as a bóithrín meandered in an extended horseshoe overlooking the main road. In between was a marshy field, with bushes and ferns and a winding stream running parallel to the main road. Off this bóithrín were two smaller bóithríns running to other roads further north. There were also two gaps in the ditch. This all meant that ready-made places of retreat were there should the necessity arise. (See Map 2). On the other hand, the enemy (should they arrive) would be walled in by a thick growth of trees, bushes and a steep, furzy hill field to their backs, while their only protection against the ambushers was a two-foot high mud wall lightly beaded with ferns.

Deasy had to secure some documents and dispatches which he had in his possession. Jackie and Tom Murray, the sons of the family, had been east of the house (Murrays', where the men had assembled for the meeting) cutting a fallen tree for firewood when Deasy called them.

"There was a safe dump under clumps of briars in the field, and Liam Deasy asked Tom to help bury documents and stuff," says Jackie Murray. Deasy sent Jackie into the house "where there was a lot of commotion." He was handed a dispatch to take immediately to the sentry across the way in Foley's house[7] where other men were billeted."[8]

Jim Kearney and Timmy Sullivan (O'Sullivan) were in the kitchen with the Foley brothers when the sentry came in with the message from Murray. He told them to go down to the cross immediately: "You're engineers, both of you are wanted; they're setting up an ambush."[9]

The two men took their cables and other equipment to the site and found that John Callaghan (O'Callaghan) had already laid a mine that traversed the main road; it was laid approximately at the beginning of the stretch of road designated for the ambush.

The ambushers stopped a Clonakilty man, Jerh. "The Leaguer" O'Brien, who was taking empty mineral bottles in a long horse-drawn scotch-car to the West Cork Bottling Company in Bandon. The car was commandeered and one of the iron-rimmed wheels was removed and thrown up on the crates of bottles. With the shafts facing east and resting on the ground, the long scotch-car was strategically placed across the road directly beyond a slight bend, so that the anticipated on-coming convoy travelling from Bandon would be brought abruptly to a halt. Jerh. "The Leaguer" was directed towards Foleys' farmhouse west the bóithrín. He was ordered to take his horse there and to remain there throughout the day.

Deasy GOC First Southern Division, Tom Crofts, Divisional Adjutant and Tom Hales, Commander gave thirty-seven other men[10]—some of whom were local Republicans who "were rounded-up" for the occasion—ambush positions in this place called Béal na mBláth (which translated means "the mouth of the flowers"). This was a small area, merely a place people passed through on the way to somewhere else. The occupied bóithrín was elevated at the north-western side and this would give the men a vantage field of fire above the spot where the convoy would be brought to a halt. Behind their backs was a narrow bóithrín leading north to Murphy's and Long's farmhouses. The men were armed with Lee Enfield rifles (.303), some also had pistols or revolvers, and a few, one being Liam Deasy, had Thompson guns. They settled down to wait—perhaps for a few hours, perhaps for the day. They didn't know.

Already, May Twomey of Cumann na mBan and a friend had been sent by bicycle to Bandon to find out if Collins's convoy was travelling further or if it appeared that they were returning directly. By midday the two girls had returned and told Deasy that the convoy had gone on to West Cork.

Some of the men who had travelled from the Clonakilty area the previous evening told Deasy that Republicans had blocked the main Clonakilty road with fallen trees. Therefore it was felt that the convoy might have to turn back sooner than anticipated.

During the day, as the men maintained their ambush positions beneath a sultry sky, people from the surrounding farm houses brought them buckets of tea and buttered bread.

The minutes ticked into hours, and so the day wore on. It was past 7.30 p.m. when a light mist began to fall upon the valley. By this time, it was obvious that the men were a little weary of waiting and they wondered if indeed there would be any ambush. Hales and Deasy consulted; Hales, aware that Collins, his friend, would be one of the targets of the ambush was a reluctant participant from the outset, and was certainly glad when Deasy suggested calling off the ambush temporarily. Deasy thought that the convoy had possibly got

76

held up somewhere and must have decided to rest at some barracks depot for the night. He walked around to the men. "From what I know of Collins he is not going to come back tonight," he said, and told his men to go to billets close by. The engineers, Jim Kearney, Timmy Sullivan and John Callaghan, were instructed to roll up the cable. "We'll have another try in the morning," said Deasy.[11]

De Valera had reached Clashbee near Mallow by this time. Siobhán Creedon[12] was in bed, having returned from work with a heavy cold, when a dispatch rider arrived with a letter from Liam Deasy asking her to go immediately to Batt Walsh's home in Clashabee, "I was to bring some form of transport. De Valera would be there so I was to arrange his accommodation for the night. The next day a blue car would come to take him over the Tipperary border because he was returning to Dublin."

According to Deasy's order she was not to give the job to anybody else but to do it herself. With her brother Michael, Siobhán set out in the pony and trap for the eight-mile cross-country journey to Clashabee. The Walsh home was heavily guarded and de Valera was having a meal with Liam Lynch when they arrived. Some of the discussion centred around Michael Collins as it was known that he had passed in a convoy through the nearby area of Whitechurch a few days previously on his way to Cork.

"When the convoy had stopped at Monee to put petrol and water in the touring car," said Siobhán Creedon, "a local man who casually asked one of the soldiers whose convoy it was, was informed it was Michael Collins on an inspection tour of Cork county." Soon the Republicans were the recipients of this information obtained from an "indiscreet soldier."[13] A dispatch was sent immediately to their comrades in the Middleton/Cobh area where some men had been billeted after the fall of Cork. The Republicans, thus alerted, mined the road the following morning before Collins was due to pass through. The discussion in Walshs' kitchen centered around the failure of this mine to explode and the ambush that had been set up in the Ballyvourney/Ballingeary area two days previously. The news from the Ballyvourney/Ballingeary area was brought by de Valera; he also told them about the decision taken that morning by the men in West Cork to lay an ambush at Béal na mBláth.

The possible reasons for Collins's visit to Cork were debated. De Valera told them that Deasy and the West Cork men were extremely surprised that Collins should travel through such Republican country and that therefore they looked on this as a challenge.[14]

Chapter 8

Dalton felt that "normality and law and order should not be too far off. We were in possession of the principal towns in Cork County. Michael Collins and I discussed this on the journey through West Cork." Much of the conversation along the route "dealt with events that had happened, there were suggestions as to the future, and there was some small talk about the countryside; whenever he was familiar with a district he mentioned this. I remember the early part of the journey as being very pleasant. He was certainly happy as we drove towards West Cork. It was a beautiful August day. Because there were still daily ambushes, I was in trepidation of what could happen, but Collins saw no danger."[1]

On the road to Clonakilty, Collins spoke about some of his former friends and colleagues who were now "on the other side." He mentioned Tom Hales whom he had visited in jail during the Treaty negotiations. Collins knew that Hales regretted that the signatories did not hold out because he regarded Lloyd George "as a bluffer." Collins told Dalton that each time he met Hales, and especially during the discussions on army reunification, Hales maintained that a "federal Ireland" would solve the problem. "He spoke of Tom Hales with affection tinged with sadness. Their broken friendship appeared to have affected him."[2]

At the outskirts of Clonakilty the convoy was brought abruptly to a halt because the road was blocked by newly felled trees. All the men in the convoy "did splendid team work in pushing aside the barricades, but," according to Emmet Dalton, "Collins was more concerned that local people would be unable to get into town the following day, which was fair day, than he was that we would get on our way." It was typical of the man who constantly had time to think of others. Hatchets and saws were taken from the Crossley tender and Collins lent a hand in the clearing operation.

Collins, "always ready for emergencies, great or small, directed the work, and took a hand in carrying it out." Active and powerful in body as in mind, "he handled axe and saw with the same vigour as he "could exhibit in the direction of affairs of the State, military or civil."[3]

One of the party, John O'Connell, was trying to break through a heavy limb with an axe when Michael Collins came over to him, "Show me that axe, boy. It's not the first time I have used one." O'Connell handed over the axe to the senior man, "whereupon the Commander-in-Chief made short work of the tree."

Having spent about an hour sawing trees and pulling them into the dyke with the aid of a wire rope and the armoured car, Collins stopped, looked around and realized that it would take too long to remove the obstruction even enough to allow them to make a pathway through. "There are plenty of idle soldiers in the area, we'll rout them out to clear this," he said, then he suggested that they retrace their movements and travel along a narrow bóithrín, familiar to him, to the town.

The convoy pulled up outside O' Donovan's Hotel, which was a meeting place for some Provisional Government officers and men. While Collins spoke to Maurice Collins and others, word spread that he was in the area, and shortly a crowd gathered. Former friends came to welcome him home. Though he was invited into some houses he declined and said, "Next time!"

John O'Connell had never been in West Cork before and now saw the hooded cloak for the first time. These pinch-pleated hoods and gathered black cloaks were the prized possession of many women in the area, worn by women after marriage and often the product of hours of tedious work in the months preceding marriage; they were an unusual spectacle to the visiting soldier. Believing that the outfit belonged to some religious community, O'Connell asked a local soldier, "What sort of order of nuns are these? Or what do they represent at all, they seem to be so plentiful?" The soldier laughed and warned him to be careful, "It's the women who do the work down here," and furthermore he said, "that's the way the women dress, those cloaks can be mighty handy and are, and have been used to hide many a revolver, and indeed many of those women wouldn't be above using one on you."

Collins and Dalton lunched in the home of Collins's cousin, Maurice Collins, then went to O'Donovan's Hotel and met some of Collins's companions of former school years. They recounted many highlights of their youth and spoke with affection of their now ageing and retired school master, Denis Lyons. Lyons, an old Fenian like Michael Collins's father, drummed into his pupils a desire for an independent nationalist policy; stories of the 1798 Rebellion got new impetus with each telling. Over lunch Collins spoke of the Fenian movement which saw Jeremiah O'Donovan Rossa—a neighbour of his from Rosscarberry who is considered to epitomise Fenianism—rise to prominence mainly in America. Ever since Padraig Pearse delivered the oration at O'Donovan Rossa's graveside in Glasnevin in 1915 his words, which inspired not only the 1916 leaders but many IRB members, were spoken of on numerous occasions. Now they were mentioned by Collins, who quoted Pearse: "They have left us our Fenian dead. And while Ireland holds these graves, Ireland unfree shall never be at peace."[4]

James Cahalane of Clonakilty remembers Collins making the link between "the Fenian idea which had lit the flame, and the War of Independence. He regarded the Treaty as the first step towards freedom. He regretted the split, but that day he said, 'It's almost over.'"[5]

Without undue delay the convoy, hailed by a cheering crowd, headed for Rosscarberry. Collins had an important call to make in this region. Two men lived around here who had been involved in supplying information to the British occupying forces during the War of Independence. (The men had succeeded in supplying the information without their action gaining the attention of any of the Third Brigade men.) Collins called to these two men; local people regarded it as a gesture of friendship, believing that Collins possibly knew them in London where they had spent some of their earlier years. Nobody yet knew the nature of their business. It is understood that Collins too was unaware of their involvement with the RIC, but they had offered their services to Collins to supply information on anti-Treaty activities. "Collins spent some time in private discussion with them."[6]

The convoy rumbled over the bridge and into the town of Rosscarbery. The loud hum of the armoured car stirred the inhabitants and brought forth the people from their shops and houses. Though this was Republican territory, most people either knew or had heard of Michael Collins and certainly showed no animosity towards him. The barracks that had once dominated the town were now a burned out ruin. (The destruction of this building on 30 March, 1921 by Tom Barry's Flying Column, meant that the IRA during that period had control over an area of roughly two hundred and seventy square miles free of the enemy. It was one of the major guerilla activities that brought praise in the form of a letter from Collins at Dublin headquarters.)[7]

Collins had a personal reason to remember the Rosscarbery ambush, because on that same night British reprisal took the form of burning Michael Collins's place of birth, then owned by his brother Johnny. The incident showed the extremities to which Major A.E. Percival and the British Essex Regiment[8] were prepared to go.

Michael O'Brien and Jerry Collins, two of Michael Collins's first cousins, were among the men rounded up to carry out the burning. "There were seven, eight or nine of us taken at gunpoint by the military. When we pleaded with them to save some of their belongings, they wouldn't give in, except they left us throw out some of the bed clothes, that was all. We had to take in straw and shake it out around the house, then sprinkle petrol on it. Percival left out the horses before ordering the dwelling and outhouses to be set alight. I cry when I think of it," said Collins's cousin, Michael

O'Brien. "Percival held us there until the house was engulfed in flames."

Michael O'Brien believed "it was possibly the best thing that was done for the cause. Because in this locality and throughout West Cork it bonded people into a united determination. They thought the episode would turn Mick Collins against Tom Barry, since after all it was a reprisal for the Rosscarbery ambush, but it only strengthened their relationship throughout the remainder of the Tan war."[9]

Collins was to remember the incident with nostalgia when he spoke to Kathy Hayes in Rosscarbery on that day; even though Kathy was a staunch Republican and friend of Tom Barry she approached him as he dismounted at the square. There she unhesitatingly told him that he should not have signed anything which still asked for allegiance to a British king. Collins smiled, "That won't be for long, Kathy."[10]

He went into O'Donovan's shop and met Anne Lehane O'Donovan, who had been in Cumann na mBan and had been a good friend of Collins's since their schooldays. Following the shake hands with many locals and a few words with his contacts, Collins once more mounted the Leyland and the convoy headed for Skibbereen.

It was a surprise for Jerh. McCarthy, the officer in charge of the Skibbereen garrison "when I saw my old friend Mick Collins walking in the yard towards me". Captain Tadgh Sullivan, the other officer in charge, was equally astonished at Collins's unexpected visit. Collins met other friends[11] and had a joke and a pleasant word for all his comrades. The soldiers assembled for the normal military inspection, after which Collins conferred with the garrison officers. According to Emmet Dalton, "He listened to their complaints, gave them advice, and assured them of effective co-operation from the Army authorities on matters which needed attention."[12]

Having eaten a meal with the men Collins was on his way out of the Eldon Hotel shortly before 5 p.m. when local writer Edith Somerville approached him. She introduced herself and the pair shook hands as Dalton, Jim Wolfe and the other escort men stood by. "Keep your armoured cars away from my haven," she said jokingly, "I can't bear to see my little island being destroyed with those monstrosities."[13]

Chapter 9

Shortly after 4.30 p.m. the convoy set out for its homeward journey, back via Rosscarbery and on towards Sam's Cross. Collins pointed to the ruin at Woodfield, with its gaping windows and rugged stone walls silhouetted in the distant field against the evening sky. "There," he said to Dalton, "was where I was born. That was my home."

The convoy wound its way "back home" to his brother's place, to the Five Alls public house at Sam's Cross. On his way in to the public house situated at the crossroads, Collins met his cousins Michael O'Brien and Jerh. Collins.

When he came in, he stood just inside the door, took a look around, smiled and said, "How's everybody?" He then approached the counter, and enquired for his brother Johnny. Michael O'Brien told him that he was "down in the field." Immediately he asked O'Brien to tell Johnny to come up right away: "I can't go down with all this army around me," he laughed. As O'Brien turned to go, Collins shouted, "How's my aunt?" Almost in the same breath he said he would go across the road to see her. Collins had great affection for his aunt, (Michael O'Brien's mother) with whom he had spent much of his younger days. She was sitting on a low stool in front of the open fire when Collins approached her; she rose and with "her two hands, she grabbed his." It was she who had encouraged him to be "a good scholar." However, the two were not left to talk about old times for long. It seemed as if everyone wanted to grab "Mick's hand."[1]

They wanted him to come across to the pub to chat with them, not about the affairs of State or army, but about the past, their past, his past. "He was a bit of a schemer in his youth," Michael O'Brien maintained, "always up to tricks.

We all went to Pike school and later we were on the altar; we'd cycle to Mass and when we'd come out our bikes would be gone. Mick would have rushed out and hid them for devilment. Then we'd have a tussle on the grass —in the church yard. He always loved to tussle—all his life, it was part of the boy in the man, even that day he seemed to want a roll on the ground. It was a measure of the fun which was within him."[2]

He had a fondness for children also and they came to him on that day. Here was the man whom they had heard their parents speak of, the man who their school teacher had told them was making history. A little boy pushed past the protective cluster of soldiers, determined to see this Commander-in-Chief so that he could tell his school pals. Collins paused in his conversation and swung round, "Well, what does the garsún want?"

"To see you, sir."

"How do you do!" A warm handshake and he pushed a sixpence into the cupped youthful hand.

When Johnny came in the door the brothers looked at one another. The elder brother who had taken his father's place as head of the family welcomed "Mick" home. The two moved aside from the crowd and talked for a little while.

They discussed the work at Woodfield. Johnny was in the process of "fixing up someplace" but was staying with the O'Briens meanwhile. The members of the family who returned home on holidays really had no definite home, but work progressed in Woodfield farm. There were reminders of the days when young Mick would trot along the furrows while his father guided the horses as they pulled the plough and exposed the sods of dark earth under which the potatoes or the grain would be planted. When Johnny told him he was milking seven cows, Michael spoke of the many times he also sat under a cow and brought in to the kitchen the frothed milk for the evening tea. "His mother was always singing songs in Irish as she milked the cows."[3]

The kitchen at Woodfield had always been a venue where patriotic exchanges took place. His father would speak of past

86

leaders, men like Wolfe Tone, Daniel O'Connell and Michael Davitt. With the neighbours the chat would eat into the night as the children sat and listened around the open hearth. Landlords' agents still collected rent and showed no mercy to those unable to pay or buy out their holding. The threat of eviction hung over many families, not least the Collinses of Woodfield. Michael was to recall this on the last day of his life—a personal reason why in his youth he disliked landlord's agents. Men who had heard the story before listened as if for the first time to the hero amongst them tell of a day when his father was sick and young Michael was sent to pay £4/6/8 rent. In a shop window in Clonakilty on his way to the agent's house, he saw a football that was marked one shilling. Secretly he hoped that the agent would give him the shilling discount—something that was occasionally done for prompt payment. But there was no such luck. The agent's response was an abrupt, "Tell your father he is a fool to trust such a small lad with so much money." Little wonder that "the young Michael whose father died when he was only six, became determined when he grew up to make sure there would be no agent."[4]

During this great home-coming day, one of his former schoolmasters from his secondary days at Lissavard was among the welcoming crowd. Collins's respect for age and learning were always high. In the intervening years the schoolboy had gained wide experience and was now Commander-in-Chief of the army. He spoke with ease to the older man of learning.

Collins was very kind to old people. They smoked clay pipes. On one occasion he sent a dozen clay pipes to the old people in the neighbourhood. During this, his last day in Sam's Cross, he received words of gratitude from some of those people who were present to welcome him. Here, he was at home amongst his own people. Every one of them had a memory of him. He knew them, he called them by name. He had come to the Five Alls with his companions on many another summer's evening in the past following a cross-country race or a game of bowling. As young lads they'd discuss the reason they lost or the reason they won. Competition was important, but winning wasn't everything. Today, with his friends and his escort he would sample a pint of the Clonkilty Wrastler. Near the counter beside the small window he stood, the boyish glint in his eye, and he told how different were "the good old days of growing up" from having to live "on your wits in Dublin."

They looked up to him. He had made it to the top in Dublin and in London. When Michael O'Brien said he saw in the paper where "he told Churchill to do his own dirty work. I said, 'Mick you were right'!" These words encouraged Collins to close his fist in front of Michael O' Brien's eyes with all the boyish roguery that he could muster. "It was clear to all that here were his roots, and it was here he was happiest."[5]

But all too soon the time arrived to say goodbye to his friends and relatives. "Don't let it be too long until we see you again Mick," came a shout from the back. He assured them it wouldn't. His brother Johnny, Michael O'Brien, Jerh. Collins and a few more relatives walked with him towards the waiting vehicles. "I hope you're travelling in the armoured car, Mick, because there's still danger around," said Johnny.

"Not at all, this is my bus," said Michael Collins, pointing to the open touring car.

"Be careful of yourself," said the older brother.

"You need have no worries about me, didn't I elude the Auxies all these years!"

He told his brother, "I'm going back to settle this thing. I'm going to concentrate on a Republic."[6]

Chapter 10

As the convoy set out from Sam's Cross at 6.15 on that dull August evening of 1922 the farewell to Michael Collins held an element of rejoicing and also of hope for peace among the Irish people. Collins had told his brother, Johnny and his cousin, Michael O'Brien "that he wouldn't rest with the settlement of the Treaty, that he would go further with the British Government once there was peace here." His principal aim was "to concentrate on ending the Civil War." He said, "The British have given up their claim on us. When we begin to work together we can help those in the northeast."[1]

For his aunt, his brother, his cousins and friends who stood outside the pub and across the road near the briar-covered ditches it was a special evening, and a special evening also for this man who was affectionately known as "The Big Fellow." To them he was not alone Commander-In-Chief of the Army but also head of the Provisional Government.[2] However, the farewell would be just another happening were it not for subsequent events. These would cause each individual to recall in detail the picture of the stately soldier's smile, his gestures, his words. Irish historical events of the period would be dated from this day. This day would be remembered as *the day Michael Collins was shot.*

From Sam's Cross it was back through The Pike and towards Clonakilty. This time the convoy weren't taking any chances; again they went through the fields, through the broken gaps which they had widened in the morning and then back on the main Clonakilty/Bandon road. Collins was as happy as Dalton had ever seen him: "He was able to let himself go, and also I think he felt things were now moving his way. He didn't say much as we travelled along the flat road towards Bandon," he appeared lost in "the myriad thoughts of a crowded and successful day."[3]

Luck was on his side when he arrived at Lee's Hotel in Bandon. Among those he met were his friend and colleague, Major General Seán Hales, Column Commander of Government Forces in West Cork and also John L. O'Sullivan. "We captured most of the towns in west Cork—Skibbereen, Roscarbery, Clonakilty, Courtmacsherry and went on to Kinsale." says John L. "We had just taken Kinsale on the Sunday and when we tried to get out of the town we found the bridges had all been blown up including the metal bridge, so with the use of some boats we ferried our soldiers out of the town, making several trips. We travelled on to Bandon as we were aiming for the Dunmanway direction."[4]

When Sean Hales and his men arrived in Bandon they went first to barrack quarters in the Devonshire Arms because Hales had some military instructions and information as to his next manoeuvres. Hales sent John L. O'Sullivan, Maurice Collins (Michael Collins's cousin) and a few men to Lee's Hotel where Michael Collins was expected to arrive on his return journey. Hales would follow shortly.

When John L. and Maurice Collins got to the Hotel the Collins convoy had already arrived. The two men announced their presence and waited outside. After a short while an officer came out and said, "Michael Collins would like to see you." Collins was seated at a table. He was warm in his praise of their achievements. The men responded to his questions on the military position, and after some further conversation, he said, "I'm trying to put a finish to this business." When Sean Hales arrived, he was warmly greeted and congratulated by his superior officer and friend.[5]

The conditions of the roads were a constant threat to the progress towards capturing areas. "It makes our task extremely tedious," said Hales. "We are almost boxed in on the eastern side as several roads are impassable." However, according to John L, "Our conversation was extremely optimistic. We all felt the war was drawing to a close."

Collins was going back to Cork on the Crookstown road which was the only road open to them "as both Innishannon and Kileady bridges were down."[6] The men told him he would be heading through dangerous country. "It's Republican territory," said his cousin Maurice Collins. "And your convoy doesn't look big enough to take them on."

Collins just shrugged and with his customary smile said, "We'll deal with them; we came that way in the morning."

In a further discussion, he told them that the enemy appeared anxious for peace "judging by feelers he had been getting during the full trip from Dublin. He was in high spirits and would be glad, he said, to see an end to this dreadful business."[7]

He rose and drew Seán Hales aside for a short private conversation. Collins proposed to introduce columns into certain definite areas. These columns would work inside a ring of posts, so that there would be no portion of the Command in any region "left without the constant presence of an operating column within a reasonable distance," thus granting all districts of the Command the security of a column that would come to their assistance in the event of an ambush or other difficulty. Hales had, a few days previously, requested a Lancia.[8] Then, accompanied by Dalton, the men went towards the door.

"Keep up the good work! 'Twill soon be over," was Collins's parting salute.[9]

Outside, a local photographer clicked his camera as the Commander-in-Chief, seated beside Emmet Dalton, was about to embark on his final journey.

(Collins had left for quite some time before Sean Hales, John L. O'Sullivan, Maurice Collins and a substantial number of soldiers marched out of Bandon towards Ballineen and Enniskeane. "We captured eighteen men on the way and took them to Dunmanway barracks. In fact we were back at Dunmanway, which was two days later when we heard of Michael Collins's death. It would be impossible for me to express the sadness, dismay and grief which fell upon us— our leader was dead." John L. remembers Hales being most upset. "Together they had been interned in Frongoch for a number of months after the 1916 Rising and were always extremely close. Another question which was left unanswered for Sean was, where was his brother Tom that evening?"[10]A few weeks previously, Collins had said in a newspaper interview, "I'd rather have Tom Hales with us than twenty others." He had also paid "a high tribute to the character of Liam Deasy."[11](Both men waited in ambush positions at Béal na mBláth throughout the day for Collins's convoy to return.)

At approximately 7.30 pm. the convoy drove up Convent Hill and out of Bandon taking a circuitous route, but the only one open towards Cork city.

It has been alleged that Collins was anxious to get back to Cork on the night of 22 August to attend a meeting to make peace with the anti-Treaty forces. However, research shows that this is mere speculation. Fr. T. F. Duggan,[12] a teacher of Greek in Farrenferris at the time, "was trying to arrange a meeting in the Imperial Hotel when he heard Michael Collins was in the area," according to his sister, Professor Lucy Duggan. "Tom O'Mahony and Florence O'Donoghue were among those who were neutral. They wanted to get something started. They certainly were involved in peace initiatives, and asked Emmet Dalton to convey their intention. But, apparently, Collins was slow to make any move. It should be remembered that this was at the height of the Civil War. As far as I am aware, there was no formal arrangement for any meeting on the night of the twenty second of August."[13]

Florence O'Donoghue had been Brigade Adjutant, and was later Intelligence Oficer in the First Cork Brigade during the War of Independence, but he took no part in the Civil war. In none of his writings is there mention of any scheduled meeting for 22 August. However he was anxious for peace, and hoped to reconcile the two sides, as he, like O'Mahony, and Duggan, was totally opposed to the Civil War.

Collins, in a letter to Cosgrave asking for postponement of the Dail, had stated his belief that by 24 August, when the

Dail would reconvene, the military "would have occupied sufficient additional posts in the South to dominate entirely the positions" in each area—this would indicate their ability "to deal with the military problem" by being free from the restraints of "parliamentary criticism."[14]

Dalton said there was no mention of a peace meeting organised for that night: "As far as I am aware Collins had no intention of compromising. He wanted me to find out further what was behind the proposals of peace. I don't think Lynch, or any of the die-hards had any intention of agreeing to the suggestion of unconditional surrender."[15]

No documentation exists, nor is there any indication, that Collins was about to make peace at the expense of abandoning the Treaty, of abandoning the Provisional government, or of abandoning the "splendid progress achieved" by his forces. He was returning to Cork for the night and would travel to Dublin the next morning.[16]

Already a light mist had begun to fold in on the evening as the vehicles wound their way along the ribbon of road that led from Bandon towards Crookstown. Despite the fact that they were travelling through Republican territory, the convoy had no contingency plan should they encounter hostilities along the way. Perhaps Collins got some intuition while driving along this sparsely populated area, or perhaps Hales's parting words suddenly flashed into mind. For whatever reason he said to Dalton, "If we run into an ambush along the way, we'll stand and fight them." Dalton did not respond. Being more familiar with ambushes and guerilla fighting than Collins was, he decided he would "cross that bridge, if and when, we came to it."[17]

The armoured car was travelling "four poles behind the Leyland which was the required distance."[18] In front the scout rider, Lieutenant Smith, led the convoy towards Béal na mBláth valley.

Having expressed to Dalton his satisfaction at the success of the trip and unaware of any hidden dangers, Collins sat back and rested his hands on the rifle which lay across his knees.

(Note: *The account of the events of the ambush which follows was compiled from a vast number of interviews of the participants on both the pro-Treaty and anti-Treaty side, and also from the available written sources.*)[19]

See Map 2 for positions and note orientation:

Meantime, further north the road at Béal na mBláth the Republicans had dispersed. Some went towards houses where they hoped to get a meal and perhaps billet for the night while others went in the direction of Long's public house at the crossroads. Most of the men either sauntered along the road or followed up one of the bóithríns.

Tom Foley and Charlie Foley had gone for the horse so that Jerh. "The Leaguer" could take away the long-cart. Tom Hales, Tom Kelleher and Jim Hurley went towards the barricade and began to move the cart containing the empty crates of bottles to one side, so that local passing traffic would not be disrupted. When they had moved the cart in near the dyke, Jim Hurley said he was going "for a bit of grub."

Hales asked Kelleher if he would join him for a drink, but Kelleher said he would perfer "a bite to eat," and would follow Hurley back to Longs' house. (This is the Long family who lived in the bóithrín at the north-west —not to be confused with Long's public house at Béal na mBláth cross-roads.)

Kelleher shouted to Jim Hurley to wait for him. Hurley stopped, and just as Kelleher reached him the sound of motor vehicles rattled the air.

"They're coming!" Hurley shouted.

South the road, the convoy headed into the Béal na mBláth valley. Suddenly Smith spotted the rolled-up cable, "Mine! Mine!" he shouted, jolted his bike around and darted back to alert the convoy. Almost immediately the sound of gunfire hit their ears.

Kelleher (north the road) looked around and, believing that Hales was trapped, yelled to Hurley, his companion, "Better

fire a few shots, Hales is at the barricade, he'll be destroyed!"
With speed the two men ran over the northern (lower) little
bridge, wheeled around and fired a few shots into the air.
Hales leaped when he heard the vehicles in the distance and
ran to catch up with Bill Powell and John Lordan. Powell and
Lordan had been chatting further north in the middle of the
road when the sound of vehicles and their companions'
warning shots hit their ears. Any second they could be
mowed down. The two men ran, leaped over the little ditch
and began to grope up the steep incline of furze and bushes.
Hales followed almost immediately. (This ditch was to the
right, a continuation of the ditch to the back of Collins's army
men, and beyond the northern bridge).

Further north the road, Pat Buttimer and Dan Holland had
been strolling when they heard the sound of gunfire. They
jumped over a ditch a little beyond the bridge, also to the
eastern side, hid behind a cluster of bushes and remained
there. (See Map 2 for positions.)

Nearer to Long's public house, Liam Deasy and Pete
Kearney were sauntering along when the sound of gunfire
made them leap to safety. They were further north but on the
same side as Powell and Lordan. The growth was not too
dense, but it took them some time to make their way to the
hilltop.

Many more Republicans were strolling on the road nearer
to the Béal na mBláth pub. Now they rushed in, joined their
companions and sped out the back.

Meanwhile further south along the road, Kearney, Sullivan
and Callaghan had been walking abreast towards where the
mine had been laid. They had disconnected the cable.
Sullivan had picked up the mine and put it on his back. The
other two men had rolled up the cable and had thrown it on
the low ditch, deciding that they would come back after they
had eaten. The three men had begun to walk south towards
the Ahalarick bridge (upper bridge—the side nearest
Bandon) when suddenly they heard the loud sound of a
motor.

"Whist, they're coming," Callaghan shouted.

95

The three men made for Ahalarick bridge and rounded the corner just as they heard the motorbike buzz past on the main road, only a few yards away. Within seconds, they heard the scout-rider shout, "Mine! Mine! Mine!" when he spotted the cable. At that instant their companions' shots (Kelleher & Hurley) rent the air.

Smith, having dashed back to the tender, warned the driver, then about-turned and sped ahead, followed closely by the tender; both drivers slowed. Were they surrounded? In the stillness of the mist and with the loud hum of their vehicles, they were unsure of the direction of the threatening gunfire.

John Callaghan, Jim Kearney and Timmy Sullivan ran for cover round the ford bend of the bóithrín just beyond Ahalarick bridge only seconds before the convoy headed into the valley.

"Drive like hell," shouted Dalton to the driver of the touring car. Men were seen running up the laneway. "Stop! we'll fight them!" retorted Collins. Immediately the order was obeyed. The driver of the tender who was just crawling by this time, saw Collins and Dalton jump from the Leyland. He halted. Instantly, the soldiers vaulted from the vehicle and tried to get into positions. Already there were resounding gunshots from a selection of armaments. Confusion struck as machine gunner McPeak pointed the Vickers gun to the left and opened fire.

Callaghan dropped to the ground and began to crawl. Kearney, who had dived beside the ditch, thought that Callaghan had been hit because at that moment machine gun fire "began to mow the furze and ferns."

Tom and Charlie Foley were coming down the laneway with the horse "when the sudden sound of gunfire erupted. Then the horse went mad," and they had "to double back on the trot."

The main road where the convoy halted was rough-stoned, running south to Bandon, north to Crookstown. On the western side of this road (facing the convoy) the Republicans had waited in ambush positions on the narrow secluded curved bóithrín all day, but during the past half hour they had been dispersing. Tom Kelleher and Jim Hurley, having fired the first warning shots, ran forward and headed further up the lower end (northern side) of the horseshoe bóithrín which was beyond where the barricade was located. They took up positions on the height. Hales, running to catch up with Powell and Lordan, jumped in beside the ditch at the eastern side, and vaulted over a low section. Eventually he caught up with Bill Powell and John Lordan further up the furzy incline.

Kelleher wondered if the enemy would move further north along the main road in the direction of the barricade. Slowly both Kelleher and Hurley edged towards the south along the bóithrín with the intention of helping their comrades. They fired further shots to distract the enemy because by this time there was continuous shooting in the distance. Some soldiers who had attempted to move north at first had now decided to move further south the road. (There were no sally trees there at the time, only ferns and bushes.)

At the southern end of the horseshoe bóithrín, Jim Kearney, Timmy Sullivan and John Callaghan had taken up positions beyond Ahalarick bridge and the ford. They were closest to the line of fire from the convoy.

Under the command of Seán O'Connell, the men in the Crossley tender opened fire with the Lewis gun. This, together with the Thompson sub-machine guns and rifles which the soldiers carried, were all quickly brought into action. They were firing at the southern end of the horseshoe bóithrín—here Kearney, Sullivan and Callaghan were positioned.

The armoured car had first moved north and halted at the point where the mine had been in position all day. Much to the consternation of the three engineers, Kearney, Sullivan and Callaghan, the cable was now disconnected. If the cable had remained unrolled, Callaghan in his crawling position, could have easily moved to the location of the exploder, where he had been all day, and so activate the mine. Had this been possible, not alone would the armoured car and its occupants have been blown up but because of the ammunition contained in the armoured vehicle, the explosion would most likely have claimed other soldiers. (When Jim Wolfe returned with me to the scene of the ambush over 50 years later, he was horrified at how near he and his comrades had been to death. From such a vantage point, overlooking the road on the north-west, he decribed it as "a perfect ambush position.")

In a war situation, soldiers fight to win. And just as the Republicans regretted their failure to blow up the armoured car, the gunner Jock McPeak in that car bitterly regretted the problem he was encountering with the Vickers gun. (A few months after this ambush, McPeak deserted to the Republicans, taking with him the *Slieve na mBan* armoured car which he manned on that eventful day.) (See Appendix 1)

Speculation has surrounded McPeak's handling of the gun, which after a short time fired only sporadically despite his having in the armoured car, two belts of .303 ammunition, each containing 250 rounds and one box of 1,000 rounds loose which were to be used for replenishing the two belts when they became empty.

This operation was his first service since he joined the army of the Irish Provisional Government. McPeak, an ex-British army gunner, lightly built and 5 ft. 6 in, in height, was recruited in Scotland. On 18 August, he got an order to go from the Curragh to Portobello Barracks where he was told to be ready for a long journey on the following Sunday morning—this was to be Collins's trip south. There should have been a relief gunner (a No 2 gunner) on the armoured car, who would refill the belt should the need arise, but no such person accompanied McPeak.

Driving into Béal na mBláth, McPeak was standing in the turret with his head out the hatch, when suddenly he saw Lieutenant Smith returning, and "a few men running" up the bóithrín, (westerly direction—Kearney, Sullivan & Callaghan). Once he came into the ambuscade, he opened fire. Looking through his gun-sights he sprayed the area from the revolving turret. The armoured car moved north, then reversed south a little; it remained stationary, moved again then settled over the disconnected mine for a short period.

McPeak aimed the gun snout with the revolving turret so that it mowed down the ferns and bushes from the shelter bank where the few men from the opposing forces were taking cover. (This has been confirmed by these men who were on the hill.)

Wolfe, the driver, then reversed the armoured car south the road past the Crossley tender, touring car, and motorbike—all of which were pulled close to the ditch. On McPeak's instructions Wolfe backed the car to the entrance to Ahalarick bridge, "because most of the gunfire appeared to be coming from this corner." He was not, nor were any of Collins's convoy aware of the strength of the enemy, which was a disadvantage for them. McPeak, now in his position as a gunner, was unable to see out the front slit-window. Wolfe tried to drive up the narrow entrance; soon he discovered that it would be impossible to negotiate this rugged track with the heavy vehicle. The armoured car weighed four and half tonnes and had only a ground clearance of ten inches.[20]

"We could get bogged down, and then we'd have a problem," said Wolfe, who realised that "if we could get in, even part of the way, we would move them quickly. Somebody shouted from the back of the armoured car, 'That could be mined.' The risk was too great." So Wolfe reversed the car on to the main road.

Meanwhile, Kearney and Sullivan suddenly realised that they might be trapped; "Have you a handkerchief?" Sullivan pleaded with his companion.

"What for?" asked Kearney.

"We'll have to hold up something [surrender flag]. If they drive up here we're finished."

Kearney and Sullivan were relieved when the armoured car reversed, and felt further relieved when the *Slieve na mBan* moved north the road; again it came close to where the disconnected mine lay. The two men breathed more easily and reloaded their guns; instantly a hail of bullets came in their direction.

Once more the armoured car reversed to get a better field of fire and remained stationary south of the entrance to

Ahalarick bridge, but by this time the shots coming from it were uneven.

Dalton called out to McPeak, "Why are you not firing?"

"The gun is jammed, Sir!"

While it may not be technically correct to say that the Vickers gun was "jammed" there were stoppages in the firing. (There was no assistant gunner on the armoured car. McPeak believes it was because there was no other machine-gunner available that day. Trained machine gunners were scarce in the National Army.) Two staff Captains had remained in the armoured car to assist McPeak, and when McPeak had finished one belt and was using the second, he asked one of the Captains to take the place of a No. 2 gunner and refill the first empty belt with cartridges from the 1,000 round box. McPeak warned that each round should be absolutely even at the caps. They should have a perfect edge and not be an eighth of an inch out. Being unfamiliar with this work, the soldier did not achieve such perfection. Consequently there were continuous stoppages, because a round had often to be removed to clear the gun.

McPeak found himself in an impossible position. Having used his second belt, he was now using the one the officer had filled and which resulted in desultory fire. But he was aware there was no real target, and he doubted if smooth firing would have made any significant difference. "I probably wasted the first belt by letting it go. I wanted to let the ambushers know that there was a machine gun; I wanted to make them keep their heads down."

He kept firing very short bursts, two or three rounds between each stoppage "until there came a lull in the fighting, I opened the hatch to get some cool air inside the turret, which was stifling. I had no sooner opened it when a bullet struck the lug which fastens the cover from the inside and sheered it off."

Several bullets from the hill hit the *Slieve na mBan* and bounced off the armoured plating; numerous others bounced off the road.

The men on the hill were not at this stage out for victory

but were anxious that the convoy should be intimidated into deciding to move on.

Michael Collins was a further distance north the road, mostly remaining in a prone position. Using whatever cover was available, he was taking part in his first guerilla ambush. Apart from being in the GPO in 1916 after some 'underground' training in soldering, Collins had never once put these skills to use. Though he was a wanted man during the War of Independence, because he was involved in intelligence against the British forces, his main task was avoiding capture.

General Tom Barry once contrasted his own life as a guerilla fighter with that of Collins. On the Dublin streets in May 1921, four of Ireland's most wanted men, Collins, Barry, Gearóid O'Sullivan, and Seán O Muirthile were returning home in a jaunting car when they were halted by a large party of Auxiliaries. "Act drunk," Collins whispered as the Auxies ordered them out. He proceeded to give a masterly performance joking and blasting while being searched. Barry, while also trying to put on an act, couldn't help but wonder how callously the Essex Regiment would treat such a performance in the fields of West Cork!

Avoiding capture on the streets of Dublin bore little relation to guerilla warfare. Collins "had this boyish mentality of soldering and possibly felt that because he had army men plus machine guns that they would 'show' them," said Jim Wolfe. Had they come on this spot an hour earlier when the cable and the men were all positioned, the outcome would have been a slaughter. But ambush positions in guerilla warfare are not chosen to favour the attacked. Dalton and some others in the convoy were aware of this, hence Dalton's command of "Drive like hell!"

Collins was in unfamiliar territory taking unfamiliar action. As soon as he jumped from the touring car he took cover in front of it, but almost immediately the car's windscreen was shattered. He then crouched further north the road, moving to his right. He was also to the right of O'Connell and Dalton, who were south of the touring car and who were taking cover in a prone position, in front of the little mud-bank ditch. From this position (north of the touring car) Collins fired at the seldom visible enemy. As firing continued, he again moved further north the road to his right, (in the Béal na mBláth pub direction) taking cover beside the Crossley tender. Then he moved further north behind the armoured car, which was at the time stationary and north of the Crossley tender. Around this time, McPeak encountered difficulty with the ammunition belt on the Vickers gun.

Liam Deasy and Pete Kearney were now some distance up a rise and obliquely behind (north-east of) Collins and his men. Because of bushy growth and the humpy hill, and their distance from the men on the road, sight of any target or even of any movement was impossible for them at this time. They took up positions approximately 400 yards north-east of Collins's convoy. Both men carried Thompson guns. While struggling up the incline they had heard the continuous sound of gunfire. "The lads will be destroyed," Deasy said, when they reached the top. He turned, opened fire into the bushes and shouted to Pete, "Come on, fire! Let's draw their fire in this direction."

Shots bounded around Collins, and when the armoured car moved south the road, he also pushed a little south. He returned the fire in the direction of the attackers obliquely opposite, on his left (Kearney, Sullivan and Callaghan) but without any definite target. Dalton was also taking what cover he could behind the little mud bank, and was just a short distance south of Collins. South the road, to Collins's left and Dalton's left, and facing the enemy on the bóithrín, were Joe Dolan and Corry and Quinn (the two drivers of the Leyland).

Joe Dolan who had moved into the armoured car at Bandon because "it was warmer than the open Crossley tender," had been sitting in the back as they headed towards Béal na mBláth. (It was over-crowded at this stage, according to Jim Wolfe.) After an action-filled day Dolan was tired; he relaxed and dozed; his rifle remained planted between his knees. At the first shots, he was jerked awake. When the armoured car halted in response to the stopping of the Leyland he jumped out and immediately put his rifle into action.

Other soldiers from the Crossley tender were scattered at intervals along the roadside, taking cover as they crawled on in an effort to find a definite target. Some had British army experience, while others had fought in the War of Independence and more had been recruited recently and trained. But most were chosen, not specifically, but to make up the number in Collins's convoy. These soldiers brought their weaponry into full play, mowing down the ferns and bushes along the bank where the few men on the hill were taking cover.

Both Deasy and Pete Kearney continued to shoot into the bushes; after some time there was a lull "down below."

"Is it over?" Deasy asked his companion.

Behind a ditch, across from Bill Murray's laneway, south from Deasy's and Pete Kearney's position, and east of (behind) Collins's convoy, eight Republicans from Kerry were hiding.

In the aftermath of the taking of Cork by Provisional Government forces, Republicans scattered and moved towards west Cork. Mike Donoghue and Bobs Doherty were among a group who had come from the Sliabh Luachra district in Kerry to defend Cork. After the evacuation of the city they walked, mainly across fields, and reached Upton after some days. Here they got food and horses.

Travelling again cross-country, they had reached an area east of Béal na mBláth and were in a field south of Bill Murray's house (where the morning meeting was to have been held) when they heard the sound of gunfire down in the valley, west of their position. They dived for cover. Bobs Doherty was about to fire a shot in the air when Mike Donoghue grabbed his rifle, "Do you want to draw them on us!" he snapped.

On the road below, the Vickers on the armoured car was badly jammed and McPeak got frustrated trying to free it.

Meanwhile back in the direct line of fire, to the west of the convoy, Jim Kearney and Timmy Sullivan were crouched side by side just beyond the curve of the bóithrín while John Callaghan was to their left. Leading off this little bóithrín to their right, and behind their backs, was a laneway going to Foley's house which ran practically at right angles to the main road. Denis O'Neill, known as Sonny Neill, and Dinny Brien had been walking up this laneway. They had gone a considerable distance when they heard the gunshots in the distance below. Believing that some of their companions were in trouble, they turned back.

Neill jumped inside the ditch and ran down the field towards a gateway obliquely across from and not far behind the position where Kearney and Sullivan were crouched. This gateway was practically at right angles to the road, and was located near the corner where the laneway branched off from the horseshoe bóithrín. He reached this position just as the firing eased, but he could hear the sound of gunfire from the opposite hillock (Deasy and Pete Kearney firing into the bushes).

Meanwhile Dinny Brien took cover behind some growth further north in the laneway and fired a few shots into the air. Sonny Neill, who had British Army experience, stood behind the pillar, loaded his Lee Enfield rifle and aimed at an enemy target.

The convoy men continued to shoot, mainly at no definite target, while bullets were now emanating only spasmodically from the armoured car which had moved south the road.

At the closing stages of the ambush (which is estimated to have lasted approximately 40 to 50 minutes in total), Collins, who had been in a prone position beside the mud bank, reloaded his gun and jumped up abruptly when the sound of gunfire coming from an area a distance behind his back could be heard clearly during a lull (Deasy's and Pete Kearney's gunfire into bushes up north-east, their motivation being to draw the fire of the convoy in the opposite direction, and so distract them from concentrating on actual targets.)

Collins walked a few steps out on the road in a north-easterly direction, and shouted a command. His voice was

Map 1
Outward and return journey of
Collins's convoy on 22 August
1922

Fermoy

Mallow

Killarney

Kenmare

Bantry

CORK

Cobh

Ballincollig

Cloughduv

Aherla

Béal na mBláth

Crookstown

Kilmurray

Copeen

Newcestown

Enniskeane?

Dunmanway

Sams Cross

Rosscarbery

Kinsale

BANDON

CLONAKILTY

SKIBBEREEN

MACROOM

Ballyvourney

Dooniskey Cross

OUTWARD JOURNEY
RETURN JOURNEY.

0   5   10 miles.

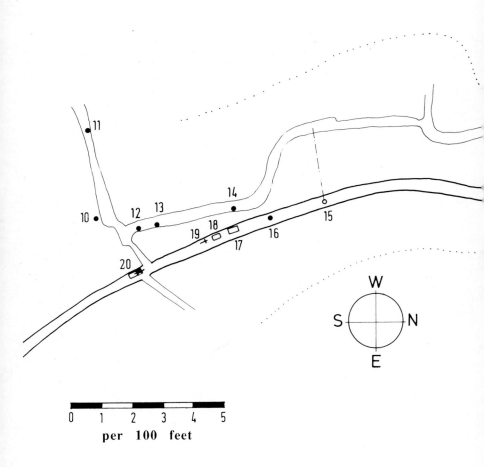

Map 2
The ambush at Béal na mBláth—detail

0 1 2 3 4 5
per 100 feet

11. Denny Brien
12. Jim Kearney
13. Timmy Sullivan
14. John Callaghan
15. Disconnected mine

16. Collins's final position
17. Crossley Tender
18. Touring car
19. Motorbike
20. Final position of armoured car

• (warning shots)
• • (attempt to draw fire from approx. 400 yards N/E of convoy)

TO KILMURRAY

TO CROOKSTOWN.

TO COPEEN.

Long's Pub.

Bill Murray's (Meeting)

Map 3
The ambush at Béal na
mBláth—general position

LONG'S LANE

marsh.

AMBUSH SITE.

N
W E
S

FOLEY'S LANE

Jim Murray's

TO ENNISKEANE.

TO NEWCESTOWN.

TO BANDON.

heard, not alone by his own men, but also by his enemy located around the ford in the horseshoe bóithrín. He was wheeling around from his right to his left, and hadn't quite completed the semi-circle when a shot got him on the poll of the head behind the right ear. He fell awkwardly and slumped to the ground. Dalton, who was not far away, thought he heard a faint cry, "Emmet!"

Sean O'Connell, who during the lull had pushed further north the road (just as Collins had done) was instantly with Dalton. They rushed to the spot.

"With a dreadful fear clutching our hearts we found our beloved Chief and friend lying motionless firmly gripping his rifle."[21]

Chapter 11

Though a mist trickled it was still daylight at approximately 8.10 on this August evening of 1922, still relatively easy to distinguish people and movements in the distance; voices carried in this valley of Béal na mBláth. Blood stained Emmet Dalton's hands as he gently tried to lift the head of the Commander-in-Chief. A huge gaping wound "at the base of the skull behind the right ear" made Dalton recognise immediately "that General Collins was almost beyond human aid." He could not speak to them.

As Dalton bent down he noticed the sound of further gunfire. "The enemy must have seen that something had occurred to cause a sudden cessation of our fire, because they intensified their own."[1]

Kelleher and Hurley who were at the north-western end of the horseshoe bóithrín began to shoot in the direction of their enemies as soon as they became aware of a lull, but because of their distance from the convoy, their vision of events and people was unclear.[2]

Liam Deasy and Pete Kearney, who were high up (north-east) obliquely behind the convoy, continued to fire "at intervals. Each of us emptied a pan of ammunition into the bushes."[3]

The men on the south-western side of the horse-shoe bóithrín (Kearney, Sullivan, Callaghan, and Neill), who could see what was happening, held their fire at this time "because" Jim Kearney said, "we knew we were outnumbered, so we wanted them to shift off." (Dinny Brien was further west in Foley's lane.)[4] Because of the suddenness of the ambush these men had been forced into this situation in a section of the bóithrín which had not been designated for ambush positions earlier in the day.

Down on the road Sean O'Connell, realising that "the end was near" for Michael Collins, knelt beside "the dying but still conscious Chief, whose eyes were wide open and normal and whispered into the ear of the fast-sinking man the words of the Act of Contrition." Collins rewarded him by a slight pressure of the hand.[5]

Meanwhile, Dalton knelt beside both of them and kept up bursts of rapid fire. Joe Dolan, who had heard Collins's command some minutes previously, had fired a few shots ahead, at no particular target, then paused momentarily. He heard Emmet Dalton's cry, "The C-in-C is hit. Keep up a heavy fire!" Instantly, he responded to the order and remained crouched.

Smith, realising that somebody had been hit, rushed back to the place of commotion. "Get him into the armoured car," he shouted; then he crouched down on one knee and fired a few shots while Dalton, still stooped, beckoned to Wolfe to bring forward the armoured car. Dalton continued with "rapid bursts of fire whilst O'Connell dragged the Chief across the road." While the armoured car jolted forward, its back doors were pushed open by Wally Coote. When it stopped O'Connell caught Michael Collins's legs and with Dalton and Smith, shifted him the few feet towards it. The blood covered cap, through which the fatal bullet had penetrated, had by now fallen off. It either fell off at this time, or had fallen off when Collins hit the ground; in any case it remained unnoticed by any of Dalton's men. With the tilting upwards of the legs Michael Collins's revolver slipped from its holster; it landed where it was to remain overnight - on the grass margin with his cap.

Aware of the dangerous position they were in while moving Collins, Commandant O'Connell endeavoured to keep Dalton covered by sporadic bursts of rapid fire. The men in the convoy were at a disadvantage as they did not know the strength of the enemy, nor did they have any idea of laneways which remained hidden from view in this unfamiliar territory. Dalton felt that there was fire coming "from that hill up behind" (Deasy and Pete Kearney firing into the bushes). He therefore gave the order: "Keep firing!"

The men had by this time got the unconscious Michael Collins slightly shielded by the hinged door of the armoured car, but he was still lying on the road beside it. Dalton had called for bandages, which were quickly handed to him by Smith. Having put down his rifle on to his knee, Dalton gently lifted the head of his dying friend and Commander, then tried to bandage it. "It was an impossible task as the wound was so large and gaping. With O'Connell's help I did the best I could and had not completed my grievous task when the big eyes quickly closed and the cold pallor of death overspread the General's face."

Still on one knee and supporting the bleeding bandaged head with the other, Dalton remained for some moments statue-like, numbed in disbelief as bullets whistled and ripped the ground beside him. "How can I describe the feelings that were mine in that bleak hour, kneeling in the mud of a country road not twelve miles from Sam's Cross, Collins's homeland. Here I was, with the still bleeding head of the Idol of Ireland resting on my arm."[6]

Shocked, Dalton kept looking at the lifeless body he now held, "the weight of the blow must have caused me to almost lose my reason." And as he wondered what to do next, he abruptly looked up and saw tears streaming down O'Connell's face. "His anguish called for my sympathy and support." Dalton took a deep breath, then said, "We'll say another prayer." Because the emotion of the moment would cause their voices to quiver, both said their few words of prayer, silently.[7]

Collins was now dead.

The fire of the ambushers had greatly abated, and Dalton assumed that they had retreated. He asked O'Connell to give him a hand to get the body of Michael Collins into the armoured car. Lieutenant Smith, the motor cycle scout who had been close by covering for them, moved forward to help to lift the weighty body. Just as they had got the body up on the platform, a bullet whizzed towards them, grazing Smith's neck.

"It was a nasty graze," said Dalton.

However, he remained on his feet and pushed the body further in towards Dalton and O'Connell, both of whom were already inside the armoured car. Then he too got quickly in. The back of the armoured car was now very crowded: as Collins's legs were not fully in, they were unable to close the hinged-door properly and had to hold it temporarily.

Dalton had given the order to mount and this order was transmitted forward. Immediately the soldiers got back into the vehicles. With Quinn at the wheel of the Leyland, it was discovered once again that it wouldn't start. Wolfe, driving the armoured car, passed back the word to his passengers to "watch out!" He had to reverse in order to get in position. The Leyland was then jerked forward by the armoured car and this got it started.

The convoy set out again, leaving Smith's motorbike by the ditch where he had first dumped it. The Crossley tender jolted the cart with crates of empty bottles (some of which were covered by an oilskin coat), breaking many and, scattering them along the roadside.

When they got around the bend and they presumed out of the view of the Republicans, they stopped. "Under the cover of the armoured car," Dalton said, they proceeded to transfer the body of Michael Collins into the touring car.

What they did not know was that high up on the hill east of them near Coleman's rock, Deasy and Pete Kearney had a view of the entire procedure. So also had Powell, Lordan and Hales—these latter three were hidden mid-way up the wooded hill. "We knew somebody was either dead or badly injured," said Bill Powell.[8]

Dalton had taken off his cap in the armoured car and used it to cradle his dead comrade's head on his lap. In the back seat of the touring car, he again used the cap to support the head, which for the early part of the journey rested against his left shoulder. This awe-stricken group thus left Béal na mBláth valley to return to the city from where they had set out over fifteen and a half hours previously.

When they left in the morning, they were "confident and happy, intent on improving the machinery of the only possible Government that could bring peace to a sorely afflicted long suffering people," according to Dalton. The burden of making other decisions now weighed heavy on his mind. He observed that "the darkness of the night began to close. We were silent, brooding with heavy hearts upon us like a shroud, the ghastly blow, known to us alone, that had fallen upon the Irish people throughout the world."

Smith was now inside the Crossley tender having had his wound dressed by one of the officers, so he was unable to guide, and in fact because of his wound, did not think about the road and the indirect route which, with the aid of Timmy Kelleher, they had taken in the morning. So the convoy followed on the straight road rather than taking the Kilmurray route at Béal na mBláth cross. Shortly they encountered their first difficulty when they came to a crossroad which was blocked in one direction. They intended travelling to Crookstown where Dalton said they would try to get a priest. Taking a right turn they wound their way until they arrived at the outskirts of a village which they thought was Crookstown but which in fact was Cloughduv.[9]

Local man, Tim Murphy was returning from a neighbour's house when the tender pulled up. Captain Conroy, the driver asked, "Where's the priest's house, we have a soldier who needs attention."

Murphy directed them towards the house beside the Church, with railings and gravel in front.[10] They stopped; one of the men got out and knocked on the door. Fr. Timothy Murphy, the curate, came as far as the railings, "and took a look at the dead Michael Collins" lying against Dalton's shoulder. "It was fairly dark at this time. I was crying, and so was O'Connell." Both men were emotionally shaken. Dalton began to speak as soon as he saw the priest. "Because I was very upset I spouted out, 'Michael Collins has been shot, I want you to help us'."

The priest turned his back to walk away. As he did so, O'Connell pointed the gun at his back, released the clip and was about to fire. Dalton snapped at it, tilted it skywards, "the shot actually discharged. Had I not jerked it, the priest would have been shot."

Dalton and O'Connell, believing the priest had refused to attend to Collins (thinking it was because the priest's sympathies rested with the anti-Treatyites) were fearful that more moves might be made to ambush them again. They got into the vehicles quickly and drove off. Filled with anguish and a sense of helplessness, Dalton wished to get back to Cork.

Because the men were crying, Fr. Murphy had sensed the sensitiveness of the situation, so without speaking he had gone back to get the oils of the dying to anoint and perform the last rites. (When I told Dalton why the priest had quickly turned around, he said, "I wish I had known all these years!" He paused, "I was so shaken at the time he turned his back, it hurt, it hurt me deeply." Over 60 years later, tears welled in Dalton's eyes, his voice trembled as he spoke between pauses. "I've often thought about it." Emmet Dalton said that years later he went back to Crookstown with his brother Charlie to try to find the Church, but the only Church he could find was overgrown "with briars and bushes." But it was in Cloughduv not Crookstown that the incident with the priest had occurred.)[11]

The day's adventures were not yet over for Dalton and the convoy. As they drove along the winding road out of Cloughduv heading in the direction of Kilumney bridge, they encountered a few felled trees, but were able to weave their way around them.

Soon those in the front of the tender noticed a man advancing towards them. Their first reaction was one of suspicion—a feeling that another ambush had been laid. They halted; every man was alerted. The stranger, when he reached them, was confronted by a number of pointed guns held by the nerve-strained men. The man told them simply that they were on the wrong road and that if they continued they would all be killed. At first they disbelieved him, "Honestly!" he pleaded with them. "Come and look!" To safeguard themselves, they took him captive. Then he guided a few of the soldiers some yards to where the road plunged. The Cork/Macroom railroad was approximately forty feet below and the bridge which normally spanned the gulf had been blown up.[12]

The man suggested that they had no other alternative but to reverse a short distance. Then they could cross over some fields and get on to the Cork road. At gun-point they compelled the stranger to show them the direction. It was a distance of three fields and a haggard.

When the Crossley tender first hit the soft earth of the fields made slippery by the evening mist, its wheels could not get a grip. The men got out and in the darkness and dampness began to push and heave the vehicle, but the wheels just spun. The engine roared; another heave was called, but again it would not move. Somebody suggested that they take their greatcoats and blankets from the truck. This they did to make a carpet. Jim Carmody pulled out some petrol tins when he went into the tender to collect the blankets and these were also used as a type of platform. Some of the full petrol tins burst and saturated still further the men's clothing.[13]

It was a laborious struggle to get this first vehicle on to the main road. The soldiers who recalled this particular episode expressed the anxiety and fear which had gripped them. They feared that at any moment there might be Republicans in the area who would seize the opportunity to ambush them (it was for this reason that they held the stranger captive until they were on their way). "We were fearful that the heavy armoured car would not make the journey" but once it got moving with the "carpet of coats" the wide wheels found it easier to negotiate the fields.

There was one more vehicle yet to traverse the fields. The touring car which contained the body of Michael Collins again refused to start. However, with the same carpet procedure this car was eventually brought to the main road. But the body of their dead leader had to be shouldered across the fields by the men. They stumbled on the muddy fields many times in the darkness.[14]

On the main road, they released their guide and drove on in the Aherla direction. In the cold and drizzle Dalton sat with the body of Michael Collins; once more he fixed his own cap beneath the bandaged head of the dead Commander and allowed the body to rest upon him in the back seat of the touring car. This car had to get another push to start, but this time they had a "fall of ground."

Collins's body now leaned against Dalton's "in the darkness rigid and dead, with the piteous stain on him—Ireland's stain—darkening my tunic as we jolted over the road. So long as I live the memory of that nightmare ride will haunt me."[15]

While they journeyed on, Dalton remembered that in the morning they had encountered some road barricades near Ballincollig. "I remember, hoping there would be no further problem, praying and chastising myself. I regretted I hadn't countermanded Collins's order, and driven like hell out of Béal na mBláth. I felt so empty during that journey back to Cork. I felt as if I too had been hit by a bullet." (During subsequent years Dalton puzzled as to whether or not he could have, or should have countermanded an order given by his Commander-in-Chief.)[16]

Luckily, when they reached Ballincollig, the trees which they had moved aside in the morning were still in the same position. The men breathed more easily as Cork would shortly be in view.

Approaching the city, Dalton thought of the priests in the Sacred Heart Mission Church at Victoria Cross, Western Road, which was on their route. The convoy pulled up on the roadside and Dalton remained seated with the body while two soldiers were instructed to ask a priest to come with them because an officer had been shot dead.

Fr. O'Brien, having promptly responded to the soldiers' call, asked them to wait a moment, then brought the oils and administered the Last Rites to the dead Michael Collins.[17]

It was a despondent convoy that arrived back at the Imperial Hotel headquarters. Their burden was great and the trials of the day had been many. General Emmet Dalton, accompanied by Commandant Sean O'Connell, Sergeant Cooney and Lieutenant Gough went into the hotel while the remainder of the convoy stayed outside. Four soldiers were detailed (two at each side) to stand guard beside the touring car which held Michael Collins's body; these men had saluted the vigorous Michael Collins in the same location early that morning.[18]

Inside, when Dalton said that Michael Collins was dead, his words were first met with disbelief. He asked Dr. Leo Ahern (Major General) to take care of the body. (After the capture of Cork Dr. Leo had taken over Shanakiel Hospital for the wounded army men of the Provisional Government, using mainly the annexe for medical services.[19]He had a team of medical men under him, including his brother Dr. Gerard. Some of the medical staff were shared with the Mercy Hospital and the severely wounded were sent to the Mercy as it had better medical facilities.)

Dr. Leo Ahern stepped from the Imperial hotel and went to the touring car. "I confirmed that Michael Collins was dead. I told the men to order an ambulance and to take the body to Shanakiel Hospital. We had efficient ambulances, each with a Ford engine—these were at the ready."

Dr. Leo Ahern drove immediately to the hospital. Commandant O'Connell who, Dr. Ahern said, "was very shocked," detailed the soldiers to go to quarters at the Victoria Hotel. Conroy, Wolfe and a few more soldiers took both the Crossley tender and the *Slieve na mBan* back to the garage at Johnson & Perrotts, then retired to quarters overhead. Commandant O'Connell and Commandant O'Friel escorted Michael Collins's body to Shanakiel Hospital.[20]

Emmet Dalton now had to attend to many necessary items. To him fell the task of informing the world that the Commander-in-Chief of the Irish Army had been shot dead during an ambush. "At the time, we were working on short-wave radio which was put together by Dowling, son of the man who was Registrar of the Royal College of Science in Ireland. First, I had to get in touch with Waterville and the message was relayed from there by cable to New York, and from there back to London and Dublin. Because of destruction caused by the Irregulars as they evacuated Cork city, there were no direct telephone links from army headquarters in the city to Portobello Barracks, Dublin, during the hours of darkness."[21]

Dalton had also "to keep in touch with and inform" the army units in various parts of the city. When he told the soldiers stationed at Victoria military barracks (now Collins's barracks) and word went around "they got into a very angry mood". The subsequent few hours were very trying as he felt he was going to be faced with a mutiny. He knew a mood for revenge was swiftly brewing. Eventually, with the aid of officers he succeeded "at gun point in getting the men to return to their units." He even found that some local officers wanted "to set out on a mission of revenge."[22]

Day was dawning when he got back to his quarters in the Imperial Hotel. It had been practically twenty-four hours packed with activity, turmoil and tragedy. He needed a short lie-down in order to focus mentally on the extra tasks, including funeral arrangements, which had suddenly fallen on his youthful shoulders. Shortly he would have to make his way up to the north side of the city to Shanakiel Hospital. "I couldn't rest. I just kept thinking."[23]

Chapter 12

When Michael Collins's body arrived at Shanakiel Hospital, the Cork "casualty clearing station" shortly after 1 am, Matron Forbes checked the list and confirmed that all private rooms were full. Dr. Leo Ahern said, "We'd better move some patient." Whereupon Dr. Christy Kelly, who had a room in the annexe suggested, "Use my bed."

The body on the trolley was examined by Dr. Leo Ahern, who then asked Dr. Michael O'Riordan and Dr. Christy Kelly to help him in carrying out an autopsy. The bandages with which Emmet Dalton had encased the crown and poll of the head had to be removed to ascertain the extent of the injury and the type of bullet which had caused Collins's death; clean bandages were subsituted. Nurses made ready the bed in room 201 where the body was then taken.

The dead Commander-in-Chief of the Irish Army was laid out in his uniform and boots. The empty holster was removed. Later it was casually thrown into a locker by one of the nurses who was tidying the room. A sixteen inch high silver crucifix (mounted on a stand) was placed on a table to the right of the body.[1] Six large "mourning" candle-sticks and candles were strategically positioned, three at each side of the bed. The curtains were drawn and the candle lights flickered and a guard of honour was mounted in the room. Dr. Christy Kelly, who had a camera in his wardrobe (this was his room) decided that he would like to have a picture.

Dr. Leo Ahern, with two officers, had already left by car for Dublin. "All communications with Dublin were cut off, so once I had examined the body and organised things at the hospital, I headed for Dublin. Arrangements had been made for the embalming; also Government officials had to be contacted so that we could await the arrival of the body at the North Wall. [2]

Around 6 a.m. Dr. Christy Kelly went to the Aherns' home at nearby Strawberry Hill. Dr. Gerard Ahern was asleep when Dr. Kelly came into his room, "Wake up! Michael Collins is dead!" he shouted. The events of the night were then related as they sat over an unusually early breakfast prepared by Mrs. Ahern. A third member of the Ahern family, Fr. Joe Ahern,[3] was one of the curates attached to Shanakiel hospital but was on holidays in Crosshaven; Dr. Gerard sent word to him, and he returned.

Dr. Gerard suggested that his colleague should go to bed in his house, but Dr. Kelly wished to return to the hospital. At 8.30 a.m. they arrived back at the hospital and went into Room 201 ("I remember the time because Kelly asked me, "What time is it?")

Dr. Kelly decided he would like another picture of Collins from a different angle. When the two men entered the room, there were just four soldiers on guard with rifles. "That's strange," said Dr. Kelly, half to himself.

"What?" asked Dr. Gerard.

"Those things on the chair," said Kelly. During his absence a greatcoat had been thrown over the back of the chair and a blood-stained cap rested on the seat. They had not been there when he had taken the first picture, nor had he seen them when the body was brought in. One of the soldiers said that these were the Commander's items. Kelly took up the coat and looked at it, then handled the cap. "What puzzled him entirely was that there was no bullet hole in it, though it was smeared in blood. It was still wet." Kelly took yet another picture as confirmation and both doctors left. (Later on in the day he took a further picture of the cortège going down Shanakiel Hill).[4]

Due to the disruption of both the railway line and roads between Cork and Dublin, a boat owned by B & I would take the cortege. The *S.S. Classic* (later known as the *Kilbarry*)[5] would be used; this had docked at Penrose Quay in the morning, having travelled from Fishguard as part of a regular

117

service, and was scheduled to embark for Dublin in the evening, then travel to Liverpool the following morning.

At 7.30 a.m. Dalton sent a wire to Portobello Barracks which was received at 9.10 a.m. (working P.O. hour). The message read:

> "To General Staff, Dublin,
> "Commander-in-Chief shot dead in ambush at Bealnamblath near Bandon 6.30 Tuesday evening with me. Also one man wounded.
> "Remains leaving by Classic for Dublin today Wednesday noon. Arrange to meet.
> Reply.
> Dalton."[6]

In the afternoon, Cronin & Desmond Funeral Service fulfilled the necessary undertaking duties. Fr. Joseph Scannell, Army chaplain,[7] assisted by Fr. Joe Ahern recited the funeral prayers. The cortège moved off down Shanakiel Hill shortly after 4 p.m., then through the city streets towards the quay.

People from Cork city and surrounds came out in their hundreds to watch the slow march of soldiers as they carried the tricolour-draped coffin of their dead Commander-in-Chief. The long procession of uniformed army men that proceeded down the quay included many of Collins's former friends and colleagues. Along the route and at the pierhead, weeping crowds knelt in prayer. Emmet Dalton observed that, "There were tears in most of the men's eyes as we took the boat slowly down the river Lee."

Soldiers stood to attention, rifles reversed, as the boat moved on its journey. When it neared Cobh the high bell on St. Colman's Cathedral resounded over the calm water. At twilight the boat drew near to Cobh. Beside the harbour, men from the British destroyer fleet stood to attention on deck. "We were greeted with a salute of trumpets from the sailors; as we went quietly on, they sounded the Last Post. " Emmet Dalton would "never forget the sight and the sound. All the windows of the houses in Cobh were lit with either candles or lights of some description—they flickered like fairy lights, and the strains of the music over the water was most impressive—so very touching. It would bring tears to a stone!"

It was a long dreary journey for the men on the *Classic* as the boat wound its way around the south-east coast of Ireland. And for the many who lined the North Wall, Dublin, it was a lingering desolate wait. Members of the Provisional Government and many of Collins's special friends remained locked in their own thoughts. "I began to think, during this seemingly unending wait, what would happen to the country now," said Ernest Blythe. "We had thought, as Mick did, that the warfare was almost finished; we felt it might be possible to reach some accommodation that would prevent this continued guerilla destruction."[8]

Meanwhile on the quay-side "drizzling rain added to our gloom," according to Oliver St. John Gogarty. Hour after hour they stood, "the officers in their uniforms blackened by rain—officers of an Irish National Army."[9]

At last a bright light was seen coming in on the water. (The time of arrival appears to have been somewhere between 2 and 3 a.m.) Grief was noticeable among those who gathered. Many who awaited the arrival wept openly. Oliver St. John Gogarty, who had been friendly with Collins since the War of Independence, when Collins used his house as a place of refuge while "on the run," said he saw women dressed in fur coats who knelt "and chanted prayers into the murky sky."[10]

Troops with reversed rifles formed a body guard as the waiting gun-carriage received the coffin which was draped in the tri-colour. Then began the procession through the streets of Dublin, bound for St. Vincent's Hospital. Ernest Blythe was among "the small procession who walked behind the gun-carriage, along the empty dark streets around 3 o'clock. There were a few people at some corners, but in the main it was just members of the government, friends, and some of the army. It was dreary. We were shocked and saddened."[11]

Gogarty, a skilful surgeon who was to embalm the body, wanted to have the task completed before noon, so he decided to have a short nap before he began work. He had just got into bed when he heard a loud knocking on the door. Desmond FitzGerald, Minister of External Affairs, was anxious that the embalming should be undertaken right away. At 4.30 a.m, Gogarty, not realising that he was still in his bedroom slippers, walked through the empty streets with FitzGerald to awaken the porter of the College of Surgeons. When they got no response at the front entrance they went round to the large gate at the back of the dissecting room. As both hammered loudly with the flat of their hands, a bullet embedded itself above their hands. While they continued to bang, there was "another plunge of lead in pine."

"Leave it to me, the job is not a lengthy one, I will come back at six o'clock," Gogarty assured the Minister. Meanwhile, he said he would try the Anatomy School of Trinity College.[12]

When Gogarty reached St. Vincent's Hospital Seán Kavanagh had just arrived. Gogarty asked him to get Albert Power, the sculptor, to come and make a death mask of Collins. With snipers active about Dublin streets during an uneasy dawn, the death mask was taken and the embalming begun. Dr. Leo Ahern remembers the skill with which Dr. Gogarty carried out the embalming. When the task was completed the body was changed to a stronger, more decorative oak coffin, so that the Nation could observe the dead hero in full glory.[13]

Lady Hazel Lavery had told her husband, Sir John, on Tuesday evening "All day I have been seeing them carrying Michael covered with blood. Wherever I go I cannot get rid of the sight." Upset at hearing this he eventually got her to go to bed then "sat with her until well on into the night, and at last she went to sleep. At seven in the morning her very English maid came in with the tea. After she had put it down, she said in a voice showing not the slightest trace of interest, 'They have shot Mr. Collins, my Lady!'"[14]

Later that morning (Wednesday) Countess Elizabeth was sitting with Bernard Shaw's wife beside the fire in the study at Kilteragh House where Michael Collins had dined with them just a few nights previously. Suddenly the door opened and Hazel appeared "in deep mourning".

"I knew it before I saw the papers," she said, "I had seen him in a dream, his face covered with blood."[15]

On Thursday morning, Lady Hazel and Countess Elizabeth went to view the body at the chapel of the Sisters of Charity at St. Vincent's Hospital, where tall candles burned at the head and feet while four soldiers "guarded him in his last sleep. Michael Collins lay in full uniform, and to him death had given her full measure of beauty and dignity, increased by the effect of that white bandage round his head, which hid the wound made by the bullet that had killed him. His face had taken on an almost Napoleonic cast."[16]When she whispered to one of the soldiers, "Where has he been hit?," he responded by touching the back of his own head. The two young women with tear-stained faces stood for some time in silent prayer and then left.

A short while later, Kitty Kiernan, the young women to whom Collins was engaged and who had expected shortly to be his wife, entered the little chapel accompanied by her sister. Tears trickled down her cheeks as she stood looking on him for a long time.

There were no words now on this Thursday morning of 24 August 1922—just some silent prayers accompanied by tears. All that day the body remained in the chapel.

When Joe O'Reilly, Collins's friend of many years (who had given him the orange drink on the night before he left Dublin) approached and stood beside the coffin, he burst into uncontrollable crying for some moments. In the stillness the emotion was picked up by those who stood around. Beside Joe, the newly ordained Army Chaplain, Fr. Sean Piggott, turned and whispered to him, whereupon Joe asked Fr. Sean if he wouldn't mind cutting a lock of Michael Collins's hair. O'Reilly had a scissors in his pocket. He took the lock that the priest handed him and put it in a concealed part of his watch.

Sir John Lavery regarded it a privilege to be allowed to paint Michael Collins in death as he had already done in life. He noticed that "the peculiar dent" near the point of his nose seemed to have disappeared.

> He might have been Napoleon in marble as he lay in his
> uniform, covered by the Free State flag, with a crucifix
> on his breast. Four soldiers stood around the bier. The
> stillness was broken at long intervals by someone
> entering the chapel on tiptoe, kissing the brow, and then
> slipping to the door where I could hear a burst of
> suppressed grief.[17]

There were many difficult moments during that painting session, moments when Lavery found the tears welling up in his own eyes. "One woman kissed the dead lips, making it hard for me to continue my work."[18]

In the late evening the body was placed in the oak coffin that was specially made, for the dead Commander-In-Chief, by carpenters who had worked through the night. The remains were ceremoniously taken to City Hall for the public lying-in-state which lasted until Sunday evening. Daily the queues lengthened, often extending to a mile long and moving slowly past the body of a man who had either directly or indirectly affected their lives. "It seemed as if all Dublin wanted to do honours to him in death."[19]

Members of the Squad, Collins's Intelligence Officers, Provisional Government members, Army officers, and other close comrades proudly took their turn to guard their dead Chief.

A black-shawled woman, one of the many from the back streets of Dublin, filed passed the coffin. For a moment she stood, and in the hushed silence of the great hall where hundreds of people awaited their turn, she cried out, "Michael Collins, Michael Collins, why did you leave us?"

On Sunday evening the oak coffin was carried to the Pro-Cathedral where it remained under guard overnight. Next morning several priests and Bishops officiated. Dr. Fogarty from County Clare had warned Collins at Griffith's funeral that he (Collins) might be next. Dr Fogarty said to a friend, "Mick didn't see danger anywhere."

Following Requiem High Mass, the coffin was placed on a gun-carriage—the gun-carriage which by a strange irony had been borrowed from the British and used under instructions by Emmet Dalton for the shelling of the Four Courts and which in a sense announced the outbreak of the Civil War.

The Provisional Government purchased four black artillery horses from the British for the occasion. And so the procession set out on the six-mile journey to Glasnevin cemetery. To the slow marching air played by the pipe band, the three-mile long cortège moved past the thousands of people who lined the route. Many had travelled from counties throughout Ireland, including a large number who had accompanied the body on the boat from Cork.

Some of those who were unable to view proceedings from the "front-line" climbed up on walls, monuments and even roof tops. Women who had picked little bunches of flowers tried to get near the bier so that they could place their tributes on it.

Most of the soldiers were unused to the polish of ceremonial drill, yet according to on-lookers, "they performed their task of the slow-march pace" by back streets from City Hall to the pro-Cathedral and from there to Glasnevin "with dignity."

Many of Collins's comrades in arms and in politics now stood at the graveside—men like Dalton, Mulcahy, Dolan, O'Reilly, Cosgrave, O'Higgins, Blythe and many others. His friend and admirer, Dr. Fogarty from County Clare, officiated at the ceremony. Army Chaplain Fr. Sean Piggott and priests from all over the world came to pay their respects. Richard Mulcahy, who would afterwards take Michael Collins's place as Commander-in-Chief of the Army, was almost poetic when he delivered the oration over his dead friend.

" ... those of us you leave behind are all, too, grain from the same handful ... Men and women of Ireland, we are all mariners on the deep, bound from a port still seen only through storm and spray, sailing still on a sea 'full of dangers and hardships, and bitter toil'. But the Great

Sleeper lies smiling in the stern of the boat, and we shall be filled with that spirit which will walk bravely upon the waters."[20]

The oration was recorded by Michael Collins's brother-in-law, Patrick O'Driscoll (a reporter in Dáil Eireann) on the blank page in the back of his prayer book.

The coffin having been lowered into the grave, and covered with soil, the oration having been delivered and the final prayers and rosary recited, it was time for all to move away. Yet, many lingered around the mound of fresh brown soil. Two tearful women met for the first time. Michael Collins's fiancée Kitty Kiernan and his dear friend Lady Hazel Lavery spontaneously embraced. Other friends sobbed softly.

To the remaining members of the Provisional Government and officers in the Army was left the task of picking up the threads of Collins's work and weaving it in their own way.

Winston Churchill, in his tribute to Collins and Griffith, said that they were two men "who feared God, loved their country and who kept their word."[21]

Chapter 13

(The following account is based on eye-witness accounts of the aftermath of the ambush, as given to the author.)[1]

In the stillness of the misty evening, the echo of gunfire which ascended from Béal na mBláth valley was heard for miles around. So when the convoy moved north the road, all was calm once more. For the Republicans that ambush was over. They didn't think any of their men were dead, or injured, but they felt there would be a type of roll-call or assesment afterwards, possibly in Bill Murray's, where perhaps the meeting which had been postponed in the morning would be reconvened. Meanwhile the men needed food. After their long dreary wait under the hot August sunshine, a wait that culminated in a swift, sharp, unexpected ambush, they were hungry.

Sonny Neill and Dinny Brien came forward to Jim Kearney and Timmy Sullivan. "I dropped one man anyway," said Neill.

"You're a crack shot," said Sullivan. "Was it you got the other lad too?"

"Yes, " said Neill. "But he jerked from me."

"It must have been our lads who were firing over across," said Sullivan.

"That's what got your man moving," said Neill.

Suddenly Kearney remembered that John Callaghan had crawled up the bóithrín when the ambush began, and now he wondered if he had been hit. Kearney and Sullivan said they would look along the bóithrín, while Neill and Brien said they would go down along the road. Neill also wanted to assess positions which had been held by the enemy, and to review the situation for himself.

As they were about to break-up, Liam Deasy arrived. He was fuming. He held a revolver to Kearney's forehead. "Why didn't you blow up that blasted mine! " he yelled. Sullivan jumped forward. "Don't wrong the man, the mine was disconnected. They were your orders, Sir."

"Alright," said Deasy.

"We got one man," said Neill.

"A pity they didn't come a bit earlier and we would have blasted the lot," said Deasy, slightly calmer. "Was there anybody hurt?"

"No," said Kearney, "There weren't many of us here to be hurt."

They told him they weren't sure if John Callaghan was hit or if he was "gone for grub." It was decided that they would all make further enquiries.

Deasy said he was going up to Bill Murray's. They could all gather there after their meal.

The men then scattered. They travelled to various houses in the locality where they expected to get food while scouts stood guard outside the houses, as had been the policy since the War of Independence.

Bill Powell had been up to the east during the ambush, in a high bushy field north/west of Bill Murray's; now with John Lordan he came out on to the road where some more men were walking. As he walked on, a bullet which accidently discharged from one of his companions' guns scared Powell and brought a reprimand from Deasy. It was obvious that some of the men were slightly tense: the ambush which had been meticulously prepared and well-organised had not materialised as planned; the unprepared manner in which a few men were forced to take on the enemy left an air of temporary disatisfaction among the men. And as Bill Powell, Sonny Neill, Dinny Brien, Tadhg O'Sullivan, Con Murphy, John Lordan and a few more men sat down to tea in Bill Murray's kitchen they began to analyse the events of the day.

"Fifteen minutes earlier and the lot would have been wiped out," said one. All agreed. It would have been a successful ambush. No wonder Deasy was angry, he wanted some success to cling to, they said. And he would have to answer to Liam Lynch. If only he hadn't ordered the mine to be disconnected "until after the grub." So the discussion continued.

Neill, who was seated to Bill Powell's left, said that at least he had "dropped one man." And they all agreed that "getting" one man showed they were still an active armed force. One enemy was as good as another to the man with a gun in his hand.

Liam Deasy, Pete Kearney, Dan Holland, Pat Buttimer and a few more men were eating their meal in the parlour.

The men in the kitchen had finished their meal when Sean O'Galvin came in. "Michael Collins was shot!" he exclaimed.

Bill Powell felt a grip on his left arm. Immediately one man in the tension-packed room jumped up. "There's another traitor gone!" Neill, Powell, Murphy, Lordan and Tadhg O'Sullivan and the other men said nothing.

Sean O' Galvin told the men that the convoy had called on Fr Murphy in Cloughduv. Afterwards the priest's housekeeper, Anne White sent the information to him. When he finished speaking a silence followed for a few minutes.

"He's dead," said Sonny Neill. "May the Lord have mercy on his soul." Then he got up and walked into the night.[2]

Liam Deasy, Pete Kearney and the other men in the parlour made no response when O'Galvin gave them the news.

Word was sent to the other houses around. Jim Kearney was sitting at table in Jim Murray's house, which was across the valley beyond the bóithrín where the ambush took place. With him were Tom Hales and some more men. They had almost completed their meal when a girl ran in saying, "Do you know who's dead! Michael Collins!" One man grabbed his cap from his knee, and triumphantly threw it up. Again, a first reaction—one of the enemy. Tom Hales joined his hands, lowered his eyes and said nothing. Then he blessed himself and remained with head bowed for some time. The other men around the table sensed the tension in the room.

Back in Corcorans' of Newcestown, Tom Kelleher, Jim Hurley and more men heard the news a little later.

Some of the men who had eaten in neighbours' houses returned to Bill Murray's where the postponed meeting was expected to be reconvened. When the group assembled, it was with a heavy heart that the men received confirmation that Michael Collins was dead. "It was only when we thought of the implications, and also when we thought of the man that it began to dawn on us the whole thing was a tragedy," said Liam Deasy. "The original purpose of holding a meeting was suddenly changed. Our meeting that morning was to decide on our future policy. We intended, with de Valera present, to consider his views. Now we felt future policy was being decided for us." Liam Lynch would have to be fully informed about the ambush.[3]

Later that night Tom Hales, Liam Deasy and Tadhg O'Sullivan walked silently down the road from Murrays' house. Over the past number of years all three had been close friends of Michael Collins, "We wondered why of all the men in the convoy did it have to be Collins who received the fatal shot. I remember we said little; we parted without discussion."[4]

Kearney walked north the road and into Long's public house where he met Tom Crofts who was with a few more men in a back room. Kearney had an exploder, also a roll of cable over his shoulder. The mood was very subdued. In Crofts's opinion: "It's not safe to stay here tonight, I feel there could be a big round-up." Kearney asked if anybody had seen John Callaghan. Nobody had. Kearney decided he would go back to the ambush site to look for him. As he walked south the main road, he saw some activity in the bóithrín. He spotted flickering matches, men were obviously searching.

"Who's there?" asked Kearney.

"Is that you Jim?" came Timmy Sullivan's voice.

"Yes, hang on," said Kearney who went around to them and asked if they had seen John Callaghan.

"We found his hat," said Foley.

As Kearney, Foley and Sullivan walked south the main road, they saw, with the aid of matches, the motor bike and what looked like a cap but they decided they would get a few hours sleep and return in the morning to investigate. After a few further enquiries they discovered that Callaghan was alright. He had left the scene of the ambush immediately afterwards. Because of inadequate cover, the hat would have given him away so he abandoned it. He had moved in the direction of the exploder as he somehow had hoped to reach the rolled up cable and perhaps blow up the mine. Fearing chastisement from Deasy, he moved away from the ambush scene as soon as it was over.

The following day Sonny Neill and Jim Kearney conversed, "I used the wrong bullet," said Neill.

"What do you mean?" asked Kearney.

"It was a dumdum!"

Kearney knew what that meant. (These were bullets used by the Black and Tans, which were picked up by the IRA, ammunition captured after ambushes during the War of Independence and retained by the men.)

Neill, who originally had two clips with five bullets in each, told Kearney he was going to dump the remainder.

Chapter 14

On Wednesday, 23 August, the day after the Béal na mBláth ambush, Liam Deasy sent a dispatch to Liam Lynch.

Lynch stated in his acknowledgement:

> Considering the very small number of men engaged this was a most successful operation, and they are to be complimented on the fight made under such heavy fire, and against such odds.
>
> Considering you were aware of the fact that the convoy contained an armoured car, it is surprising you had not mines laid to get this.[1]

There *was* a mine laid, and, as has been established, it had been disconnected before the convoy arrived. Why then did Deasy not inform Lynch of this?

"This was just a brief dispatch. Lynch was informed afterwards of the full facts."

Liam Lynch believed that the stand the Republicans had taken was correct, but in his acknowledgement he regretted that "nothing could bring home more forcibly the awful unfortunate national situation at present than the fact that it has become necessary for Irishmen and former comrades to shoot such men as M. Collins who rendered such splendid service to the Republic in the last war against England."[2]

Lynch had no intention of talking peace. He wrote: "It is to be hoped our present enemies will realise the folly in trying to crush the Republic before it is too late."[3]

A few weeks before his death, Collins had been equally adamant, "When the Irregulars—leaders and men ... give up their arms and cease their depredations on the persons and property of Irish citizens, there will be no longer need for hostility."[4]

Both sides had continued to fight for what they saw as "Ireland's future." A few days after Collins's death, Frank Aiken wrote to Mulcahy expressing his sympathy, despite having been "in arms against him lately. My sorrow for his death is greater because I believe that in a month or so he would have seen that he was on the wrong side, and I don't believe he who most of all was responsible for building up the strength of the nation would—when he saw that he could not win out—have disappointed that strength in a hopeless struggle."[5]

Because of the strong beliefs of people on both sides, there was a determination to win. On the day the ambush was planned at Béal na mBláth, another was being organised on the Cork/Fermoy road near Watergrasshill, because this was the road the Republicans in that area felt that Collins would travel back.

So Collins was at risk from several ambushes during his trip south. There was every possibility that he would get killed during one of these ambushes. Yet the bullet which took his life at Béal na mBláth has aroused controversy, mainly because of the large wound in the back of his head behind the right ear, at a time when it was believed he was facing his ambushers. This has led to several different theories:

> —that he was hit from behind by one of the Republicans who were returning to Kerry
> —that he was killed by a member of his own convoy, either by a close range bullet from a Mauser pistol or by a bullet from the armoured car
> —that the fatal wound was caused by a ricochet bullet
> —that a bullet fired by a Republican killed Collins.

Because the type of wound Collins received has never been confirmed, these theories require analysing. But first it is necessary to establish Collins's position when he was fatally hit.

The road where Collins and his men were engaged in ambush was in a valley. During the final stages of the ambush, after Collins had got up from his prone position, turned to his right, walked a short distance north/east the road, he wheeled around and gave an order. (His back was now to the men on the horseshoe bóithrín.) Dalton says that during the ambush, "there was gunfire coming from the direction facing us, coming from our left." [horseshoe bóithrín] "There were echoes, but I had the awful feeling that there was fire coming from somewhere behind us—back over to the right of my prone position." (This was Liam Deasy and Pete Kearney up north/east firing into the bushes.) It appears that Collins moved, and turned when this gunfire could be heard more clearly during a lull. (See Map 2.)

According to accounts given by Corry and O'Connell and several other men at the scene, Collins stood out when he gave the order and began firing. (It is not clear what his exact words were. O'Connell thought he shouted, "Come on boys! There they are, running up the road."[6] Jim Kearney, up west on the horseshoe bóithrín, thought he shouted, "Cut them off on the right."[7] Timmy Sullivan, on the horseshoe bóithrín, wasn't quite sure, but thought he shouted, "Get them on the right." or "Up there to the right!"[8] Dalton heard him shout something like, "There on the right!" and says he may have been standing when he gave the order; but when he next saw Collins, he was in a prone position. Dalton says, "he may have been falling at the time, because when I observed him he had been hit —just after this I barely heard my name being called."[9]

The bolt of Collins's rifle had been drawn at the time when he was hit, showing that he was ready to fire. He was approximately 170 yards in front of the *Slieve na mBan* armoured car (the armoured car was, at this time, south the road beyond Ahalarick bridge) and he was approximately 175 yards from the turn in the horseshoe bóithrín around which Kearney and Sullivan were positioned a few yards apart and where Callaghan had moved further north. Collins was 185 yards from the further pillar of the gate, inside which Sonny

Neill was positioned. From this position (Neill's) there was only a slight elevation, of approximately four feet. Collins was close to the point where the river flows nearest the road,[10]and was approximately five feet out from the dyke (water-channel).

Because Collins had turned and was facing the direction in which the Kerry men were hiding, they could not have hit him in the back of the head with a bullet. These men had no view of a definite target, and in order to preserve their own safety they did not fire any shots. Therefore this theory can be ruled out.

The theory that there was a traitor in Collins's convoy who saw the opportunity and decided "to get him" at an appropriate moment will now be examined.

It was only on Friday morning 18 August that Collins asked Joe McGrath, Director of Intelligence, to organise the convoy. No advance warning was sent to Dalton in Cork, though Collins did inform O'Duffy.[11]Fionán Lynch believed that Collins was unsure whether or not he would get further than Limerick, though his intention was to go to Cork. Also, for security reasons each stage of the journey would be decided at Collins's own discretion. Therefore it was Joe McGrath who was responsible for the men delegated to escort Collins. So if there was "a plant" among Collins's escort men, he would need the co-operation of Joe McGrath, who would in turn need the co-operation of Captain Coghlan, because Captain Coghlan was "the Army man" in Portobello Barracks with whom Joe McGrath liaised in selecting the men, the transport and the ammunition for the journey.

Certainly, Collins was annoyed that the transport was not perfect, he was also displeased with the "unprepared escort."[12]They were "not as lively as he would have wished and they were unused to conditions along country roads," according to Dalton." [13] But there is absolutely no reason to think that Collins suspected their loyalty. The men who were detailed to escort Collins appear simply to have been men who were available in Portobello Barracks at the time. Ernest

Blythe said, "Many of the good fighting men were in action in other parts of the country, the men picked for the journey south were in action in Dublin."[14] There is no evidence to doubt the integrity of Joe McGrath or of Captain Coghlan.

So, still supposing there was a "plant" and by some coincidence he happened to be picked, or got himself selected for the tour, then he would have to wait for the opportune moment to do "the job."

But if the Republicans had not seen a Provisional Government forces convoy passing through "their" area, on the morning of 22 August, then there would have been no ambush set up; they planned the ambush because all other routes to Cork were blocked, which meant that this convoy would have to return through Béal na mBláth.

Also, if Collins's convoy had been a half an hour later on its return journey, there would have been no ambush. When then, would "the plant" have done "the job?"

But to carry the supposition to its ultimate by suggesting that all things were working in favour of the alleged "plant" and that luck was on his side, was he in the right place to do "the job?"

The position Collins was in when he was killed has been established. He had distanced himself from his comrades and had turned his back to the ambushers when he was hit. At this time he was approximately 170 yards in front of the armoured car, in view of the driver, Jim Wolfe and his co-driver Wiggy Fortune. He was the man who was at the extreme northern end of the convoy. If "a job" was to be done, it would have to be a clean one, so a Mauser pistol would be used; this would mean an entry and an exit bullet wound which would have been inflicted when the shot was fired at a fairly close range with Collins about to wheel around. The "plant" would have to be close to Collins at the precise moment to inflict the fatal wound. A blunder would be disastrous! This would mean that the killer would have to follow Collins's movements during the ambush. The killer would have to risk being seen by other members of the convoy, including the men in the armoured car.

Jim Wolfe, the driver of the armoured car, concentrated his gaze through the small slit-window, as his job was to move when machine-gunner, McPeak, wanted him to or when the necessity arose. Looking on the road ahead he could easily see any irregularity. Co-driver Jimmy "Wiggy" Fortune was in a similar position. Jim Wolfe saw Collins a distance in front of the armoured car when he was hit. "He was down from us. We had moved up from him. He was out on the road when he swung round. I saw him fall rather awkwardly." (down=north; up=south.)

"Was he with somebody, or on his own?" I asked.

"He was on his own at the time," said Wolfe.[15]

As Collins seems to have been standing alone when he was hit, there is no evidence to show that a close range Mauser bullet killed him. If he was hit by a Mauser bullet, it would have created a small entry wound in his forehead and a large exit wound in the back of his head. So suppposing that during the course of the ambush the alleged killer succeeded unnoticed in getting close to Collins, then the wound/wounds would establish the calibre of the fatal bullet. But before investigating the wound/wounds we will need to analyse the actions of Jock McPeak who manned the Vickers gun in the armoured car that evening, because it has been alleged that Collins was shot by a bullet fired by McPeak.

McPeak had enlisted in the Argyle and Sutherland Highlanders of the British Army in 1915 but was transferred to the Machine Gun Corps on its formation in 1916. Wounded at the Somme, he was sent on his recovery to Palestine, where he served until July 1919. When he was discharged, he returned to his native Glasgow. Like six million more soldiers, he was unemployed upon being demobbed. This son of a Tyrone man was in sympathy with the Irish cause and deplored the actions of the Black and Tans in Ireland. Consequently he became involved in securing arms for the Irish cause. At a meeting with some others to make arrangements to get the cargo across the water, he was arrested and sent to Barlinie prison, where he remained as a political prisoner until the Treaty was signed.

When the Provisional Goverment was recruiting in Scotland, McPeak enlisted and came to Ireland to join the Army. "To us, it was still the IRA, we didn't know there was any difference at that time between them and the Free Staters. All we had been told was that they wanted soldiers." Shortly after he and his comrades landed in Ireland, the Four Courts was attacked, and the Civil War began.

McPeak was stationed first in the Curragh and afterwards in Portobello Barracks where the armoured cars were housed. On 18 August, he was detailed for his first service operation with the Provisional Goverment forces, as gunner on the *Slieve na mBan* armoured car. He was awakened early on Sunday 20 August, and given instructions to "get ready and stand by." His brief was "to escort Michael Collins" (whom he [McPeak] had admired since coming to Ireland) on his southern tour of inspection.

After the funeral of Michael Collins, gunner Jock McPeak returned to Cork and resumed escort duties in the armoured car for General Emmet Dalton and General Tom Ennis. Then, three months after *the day Michael Collins was shot,* Jock McPeak deserted to the Republicans, taking with him the *Slieve na mBan* armoured car. Because of this incident, because of his background, and because of the stoppages which occurred in the machine gunfire during the ambush, there has been speculation that he was a mercenary "planted" in the Collins convoy.

However if we look at McPeak's situation, it is clear that he would have had great difficulty in firing "a single shot" in Collins's direction—apart from the physical awkwardness of deliberately singling a machine-gun shot, it would have been impossible to do it without being noticed. He would have had to revolve the turret quickly to a 90 degree angle at least, thus risking the lives of many more of his own comrades north the road from him, who would then be within his line of fire. (See Map 2 for final position of armoured car.)

During the action Dalton questioned the stoppages. Therefore, it is highly unlikely, indeed it can be denied categorically, that a trained gunner would take such a calculated risk under such circumstances. Furthermore, when he deserted to the Republicans and took the armoured car with him, McPeak talked to the men on whom he had fired. And according to both Timmy Sullivan and Jim Kearney, "he fired to kill," was how he had put it. Even the mown down ferns and bushes, which the men viewed in daylight the morning after the ambush, bore testimony to the fact that he was doing a job to the best of his ability.

Because McPeak had the hatch closed he didn't know that anything had happened until one of the drivers said, " Collins has been hit."

To conclude this analysis, Jock McPeak did not shoot Michael Collins deliberately. If there was the million to one chance that he accidentally fired a shot which proved fatal, it would easily have been noticed in the same way as a deliberate shot. Someone would surely have witnessed such a clumsy operation.

Was Collins killed by a ricochet bullet? It has been alleged that bullet marks on the turret of the armoured car (now held in the Curragh) can substantiate a claim that a bullet fired from a particular position ricocheted off the armoured car and hit Collins. This can be discounted because the gun and turret which are now attached to the *Slieve na mBan* armoured car are not those which were on the armoured car on the day Michael Collins was shot (as has always been believed).

After the stealing of the armoured car, the Republicans removed the gun and turret to make it ineffective when they failed to obtain tyres for the car. These parts were not on it when it was recaptured by the Free State Army. (See Appendix 1.)

Furthermore, it is evident that a bullet hitting the armoured car and bouncing off it, would be unlikely to hit Collins, in view of the distance between the car and Collins.

However, a bullet could have ricocheted off the road and inflicted the fatal wound. If a bullet came from the horseshoe bóithrín direction (Republicans) and bounced as Collins was turning, it could have hit him in the poll of the head behind the right ear (the location of the fatal wound), because he was wheeling from right to left.

Collins wore an officer's cap. This cap was made of superfine (wool) so a ricochet bullet, (which is an indirect shot) would penetrate, blow open the skin, and create a large wound. The ricochet theory has found much favour among writers and historians.

Next we will examine the theory that Collins was shot by a bullet from a Republican's gun.

At Béal na mBláth on that day most of the Republicans had Thompson sub-machine guns. Of the five men who actually participated in the ambush directly, John Callaghan had a Peter-the-Painter, Timmy Sullivan had a Colt revolver, Jim Kearney had a Parabellum. These men were engineers in charge of the mines. Sonny Neill and Dinny Brien, the two men who returned, had Lee-Enfield rifles. After the ambush Sonny Neill was certain that a dumdum bullet from his Lee-Enfield rifle killed Collins. This was a long range shot (approximately 185 yards) which was said to have hit Collins as he turned round. Sonny Neill was the only man in the Republican party who claimed to have hit any member of Collins's convoy.

So it must now be established whether the bullet which killed Collins was:

—a bullet from a Mauser pistol
—a ricochet bullet
—a dumdum bullet from a Republican's Lee-Enfield rifle

Before any conclusion can be reached about how Collins was killed, certain very important questions must be asked:

—How large was the wound at the back of the head?
—Was there a forehead wound?
—What was the calibre of the bullet that killed Collins?

Dr. Leo Ahern was the first doctor to examine Michael Collins's body and pronounce him dead. "The wound was a large gaping wound to the right of the poll. There was no other wound," he said. " There was no exit wound … only the large entrance wound. There was definitely no wound in the forehead." He stressed, "It was important for me to check the wound, and to establish the cause of death. Therefore the wound was thoroughly checked, as was the entire head area … an autopsy was carried out on the body of Michael Collins."[16]

Dr. Michael Riordan was detailed by Dr. Leo Ahern to examine and prepare the body. When he examined the body on the trolley in Shanakiel Hospital, he noted a large bullet wound behind the right ear. "There was no exit wound. I'm certain there was only one large, deep wound … Part of the head was blown off. Some badly-stained bandages were replaced."[17]

Dr. Christy Kelly, who was present during the second thorough examination, confirmed seeing "a huge wound, with part of the poll blown off, at the right hand side. It was an ugly wound."[18]

Dr. Gerard Ahern, who was not present for the examination, but who was at the hospital later in the morning (8. 30 a.m. Room 201) said, "Dr. Kelly told me that the wound was massive—a big hole behind the right ear."[19]

Dr. Cagney, who was in the Mercy Hospital at the time and who also .attended patients in Shanakiel Hospital, did not examine the body, but was told that it was an extremely large wound, "at the right-hand side of the poll."[20]

When the body was being embalmed by Dr. Gogarty, Dr. Leo Ahern was also present. Dr. Gogarty said later that he felt the wound was caused "by a ricochet bullet.[21] The extent of the wound in the poll was not fully examined by Dr. Gogarty. Dr. Leo Ahern remembers "distinctly" Dr. Gogarty asking him "if there was any other head wound, and I told him there wasn't. He checked the forehead for marks while I held the bandages."[22] Consequently, in Gogarty's writings there is no mention of Collins having a forehead wound. Ulick O'Connor in his biography of Gogarty, has written, "With fine skill, he was able to hide the gaping wound in the back of the head and preserve in the dead man's face something of the nobility it bore in life."[23]

Therefore the theory that the bullet was inflicted by a Mauser pistol at close range can be ruled out because there was no forehead entry wound. "The entry wound was in the back of the head and there was no exit wound."

In view of Dr. Leo Ahern's army experience and also his medical experience in an army hospital, I asked him what type of bullet did he think had caused the wound? "It must have been a flat-nosed—a dumdum" (expanding). The wound was too great, and too much of the head matter had been blown off, there was "too much skull fragmentation," to have come as a result of a ricochet, he felt.

Dr. Christy Kelly who examined the body in Shanakiel Hospital that night, told Dr. Gerard Ahern that "the large wound and shattered bone-structure" was consistent with "the bloody awful" result of a dumdum bullet. Dr. Gerard Ahern said that in later years they discussed the extent of the wound. "We knew dumdum bullets were used by the Irregulars, and while we didn't say anything publicly, we were, I would say, convinced that it was a dumdum that killed Collins."[24]

In a television interview with Cathal O'Shannon Emmet Dalton said "It could only have been a ricochet or a dumdum" which caused the wound. "There was no entrance wound, it was just a great gaping hole at the back of the head."[25]

Dalton went into great detail to describe the wound to me. When asked which was the most likely cause, he said, "on balance a ricochet wound would be more surface." Yet he could not be sure as he did not examine the wound, but said this was done by the doctors.

Why was there no inquest held? "There was no necessity for an inquest at the time," Emmet Dalton believed. "Michael Collins was shot by an enemy bullet, whether this was a bullet that ricocheted or whether it hit Collins directly. There was no question but that he was killed in an ambush by Irregulars." Dalton said, that, "despite all the speculation and conjecture there was no entrance wound, only that gaping hole behind the right ear. I should know, I had him resting on my lap. It is only as the years have progressed that speculation and a question mark" has hung over Collins's death. (When Dalton speaks of the absence of an "entrance wound," he is making clear that Collins had no forehead wound, thus discounting the theory that there were two bullet wounds.)

Whatever the causes of such speculation, controversy and insinuation certainly evolved over the years. Jock McPeak has said, "I suppose every man in a way, felt more or less responsible that the Commander-In-Chief should have been killed while the rest of us escaped without a scratch—except the motor cycle out-rider, Lieutenant Smith."[26]

Dr. Leo Ahern, who spent most of his life in England, having left Ireland shortly after the end of the Civil War, "when jobs were difficult to find in Ireland," said he never had any doubt, and saw no reason to question the source of the bullet. "The effect, as far as I was concerned, told the story." It should be noted that Dr. Ahern called the wound an entrance wound — he did not know what position Collins was in, in relation to the ambushers, when the bullet hit him.

So is there further evidence to prove categorically that there was no forehead wound, only a large wound behind the right ear covering the poll area?

The final piece of evidence depends on Michael Collins's cap.

Controversy has surrounded the cap, which is in the National Museum, Dublin. The mud-stained coat and the cap in the mahogany case were sent to the Museum on 27 January 1923. Mr Oliver Snoddy, Assistant Keeper in the Museum, has stated: "The cap here is that which was sent to the Museum from Mr. Cosgrave's Office as being that worn by Collins at the time of his death."[27]

Dalton believed that the cap in the Museum was his own cap which supported the wounded head on the return journey to Cork. (How it acquired the hole in it he could not say.) He knew Michael Collins's cap and gun were left behind, so also was his own gun.

Most Republicans in West Cork believed the cap in the Museum was Dalton's because they knew that the cap which was found at Béal na mBláth on the morning after the ambush had been buried. However the cap in the Museum, stated to be that worn by Michael Collins, has a large jagged hole in the back right side, it is minus the badge, the diamond and the chin strap. This cap has all the markings of the one which was buried in Jim Murray's field by Tom Hales, Jim Kearney, and Timmy Sullivan the morning after Michael Collins was shot.

"The circumference of the leather band inside the army cap, said to be that of Michael Collins, is twenty and a half inches approximately."[28](Measurements given to me by Oliver Snoddy.)

Another cap in good condition, belonging to Michael Collins, is in the Brother Allen Museum, Dublin. This cap measures twenty-two inches approximately.[29] Collins himself handed over his own cap and a Sam Browne belt to be put on the coffin for the burial of Dick McKee on 24 November 1920. (Dick McKee, Peadar Clancy and Conor Clune had been arrested on 20 November 1920 and following the events of Bloody Sunday, 21 November 1920, these men were shot in dubious circumstances while in police custody.)

Jim Kearney, who took part in the ambush, was one of the men who found the cap, and was involved in its burial on 23 August 1922, travelled to the National Museum for the first time on 30 July 1973. Mr. Oliver Snoddy allowed both of us to examine the cap at close quarters. Jim Kearney felt certain, "This was the cap we buried." This was the cap from which he himself had taken the chin strap and Tom Hales had taken the front badge with diamond. This cap, with these parts missing, has a large jagged hole in the right back, to the right of the back stitching in the area which would have covered the poll of the head. The inside leather band has remained intact, but is rather hard and shows shrinkage. There is no evidence that a bullet penetrated the front of the cap; there is no front entry mark.

This cap bears every resemblance to the one that Collins

wore at the time he was shot; is it then the same cap?

Dr. Christy Kelly discovered Collins's holster in his locker in Room 201, Shanakiel Hospital a few days after Collins's body had been taken to Dublin. He gave the holster to Dr. Cagney who passed it on to Edward C. Smith,[30]who in turn took it to Dublin and gave it to Brother Allen. It is now in the Museum that bears Brother Allen's name.

The gun on the *Slieve na mBan* armoured car, which was removed from it after the Republicans got the vehicle, was held by them, and is now in private hands. (See Appendix 1.)

Collins's revolver was held by the Republicans and is in private hands. A revolver with the initials E.D. (Emmet Dalton) was found later in the dyke of the road at Béal na mBláth, and is in private hands.

Collins had a large head, so if the cap in the National Museum and the one in the Brother Allen Museum belonged to Collins, why is there a difference in measurement? Who originally owned the cap in the mahogany case?

The officer's cap which was buried beside the tree in Murray's field in Raheen, "contained almost a basin full of human matter," according to Jim Kearney. Some days later Jim Murray dug it up because he had cattle and some pigs in this field. "My father was afraid the pigs would nose it out of the ground," said Pat Murray. "In any case he didn't want it around. He knew it was Collins's cap." Having washed it in a bucket of water Murray put it to dry on a ditch beside the house. By this time the blood and residue of human matter was washed off. The cap remained there to dry for some days, beneath the August sun. "When it was fully dry my father brought it in, and put it in a closet under the stairs. It was left there for a few weeks. By then it had shrunk. I remember my mother stuffed it with papers and she tried to put it back in shape."

"The Stations" (a local term for the celebration of Mass in the house) were being held in Murray's household towards the end of September.[31] Because Jim Murray disliked having this cap in the house, he introduced the subject to Fr. Denis

Bernard, parish priest and Fr. Jeremiah Coakley, curate, during breakfast. Fr. Coakley agreed to take the cap home with him and held it for a few weeks. Then his housekeeper Nell O'Sullivan agreed to take it into the Free State headquarters' officer, Liam Daly, in Bandon. General Seán Hales, T.D. happened to be in the office in Lee's Hotel when Nell O'Sullivan entered. "Mick's cap," he said, "then," according to Nell O'Sullivan, "he bowed his head and remained silent."

Both men were informed of the circumstances in which Seán's brother, Tom (Republican side) had buried the cap. Seán Hales kept the cap until he was returning to Dublin. He then "handed it over to the authorities," who had also taken Collins's coat. W.T. Cosgrave was informed of the details. After Seán Hales was shot on 7 December 1922, the cap was sent to the National Museum. W.T. Cosgrave's private secretary Mr. Banim "was the person of contact" with the Museum, and " no files were sent with it" on 27 January 1923.[32]

The leather band in the inside of this cap was made of calf skin and the material of these officers' caps was superfine wool (hand-woven), according to the Military Archivist, Commandant Peter Young. These were supplied by Callaghan's of Dame Street (now Brown Thomas).

Both calf-skin (leather) and wool will shrink when dried in the heat of the sun after having been buried in soil and immersed in water. People in both the wool and leather trade have said that "shrinkage is certain under such conditions." This would allow for the difference in size between the cap in the National Museum and the one in the Brother Allen Museum. Fr. Coakley told John Joe O'Sullivan that the tear in the cap had the jagged marks of a bullet — just the one hole in the back.

It is now certain that the cap in the National Museum is the cap which was worn by Michael Collins on the day he was shot at Béal na mBláth. The cap supports the fact that Michael Collins had "one large wound " behind the right ear. Therefore, it is evident that Collins was killed by a bullet which originated from enemy lines. Sonny Neill, one of the ambushers, had his Lee-Enfield rifle aimed at the head of a man on the road. Neill's shot knocked that man—Jim Kearney, Timmy Sullivan and John Callaghan as well as Sonny Neill himself saw him fall. The bullet in Neill's Lee-Enfield rifle was a dumdum—a flat-nosed bullet. This type of bullet, according to the evidence of the doctors who examined Collins, would expand when it hit the poll of the head (bone structure). The wound caused by the bullet which hit Collins's poll is consistent with a dumdum bullet impact. The large open wound and the bone fragmentation in Collins's head show that the wound could not have been caused by a ricochet bullet.

The doctors confirm the cause of the wound and the calibre of the bullet which killed Collins. Their evidence corroborates the information which has emerged from my investigation into his death.

Seán Hales, in a statement to Seán McGarry in December 1922, said: "They knew they had killed an officer of high rank."[33] Liam Deasy confirmed: "We knew it was Sonny Neill's bullet!"[34] All the Republicans who had assembled in ambush at Béal na mBláth on the day Michael Collins was shot, afterwards knew who shot him.[35]

—Michael Collins was not shot by a bullet from a Mauser pistol.
—Michael Collins was not killed by a ricochet bullet.
—Michael Collins was shot by the Republican who said, "I dropped one man."

George Bernard Shaw wrote in a letter to Hannah Collins, Michael Collins's sister:

How could a born soldier die better than at the victorious end of a good fight, falling to the shot of another Irishman, an Irishman who thought he was fighting for Ireland—"a Roman to a Roman?"

Postscript

Whatever hope there had been of bringing a swift end to the Civil War died with Michael Collins's death. In Kilmainham jail on the night of 23 August 1922 Tom Barry noticed a questioning silence when news spread of Collins's death. Shortly afterwards he looked down from the corridor above "on the extraordinary picture of about a thousand kneeling Republican prisoners spontaneously reciting the Rosary aloud for the repose of the soul of the dead Michael Collins, Commander in Chief of the Free State forces." He felt there was little logic in such an action but it was a wonderful tribute to the part played by a man who had worked tirelessly in the struggle to gain independence for Ireland. Even through all the bitterness of Civil War "those Republican prisoners remembered that the dead leader, latterly their enemy, was once the driving force and the inspiration in their struggle against the British forces of occupation."[1]

Richard Mulcahy now took over Collins's position as Commander-In-Chief of the National Army and also held his post as Minister of Defence. As the weeks progressed the Civil War conflict continued to divide the two groups who blamed each other for wrecking Ireland's future, while many people who had remained neutral on the Treaty issue tried to set up a platform for negotiations. In Cork Emmet Dalton endeavoured, in association with Tom Ennis, to find a peace formula. But Liam Lynch, Executive forces Chief of Staff, treated these moves with suspicion. Dalton, acting on instructions from Richard Mulcahy, was anxious "to make an effort towards ending the present needless strife on the basis of an unconditional surrender."[2]

Dalton wanted the Civil War to end, especially after

Collins's death. "I was really sick of it all," he said, especially when he saw "the turn events were taking" with reprisal killings as the weeks progressed.[3]

The Republican deputies did not attend the new Dail which met on 5 September with Cosgrave as President. However, de Valera was extremely anxious to bring both sides together and to pursue his aim through political means. In his efforts to find a basis for peace he wondered if there was any method by which the Treaty decisions could be revised. But Mulcahy informed him that the Treaty was not negotiable.

Control of the anti-Treatyites was now almost totally outside de Valera's influence and he was compelled to do as Liam Lynch suggested. "The fight must go on until there is no question of forcing Ireland into the British Empire, by the enemy, foreign or domestic," Lynch wrote.[4]

By the end of September, Republican casualties had mounted to more than 300 killed or wounded and there were over 6,000 prisoners either in jails or internment camps. Provisional Government casualties up to the middle of September were 185 killed and 674 wounded. The Provisional Government issued a proclamation on 7 October giving effect to a decision to set up military courts with powers to inflict the death penalty.[5]

On the 16th of the month the Republican Executive attended a meeting in Nugents' house, Ballybeacon, near Fermoy, Co. Cork. Liam Lynch, who presided, read a memorandum from de Valera which suggested that if a decision was taken at the meeting to continue the fight, then the possibility of setting up a Republican Government which would co-ordinate efforts and prevent a Free State Government from establishing itself, should be considered; it would also mean laying claims to any funds or resources of the Republic. He stated that the only public policy necessary was to maintain the Republic and the sovereign independence of the nation.

After lengthy discussions, the members of the Executive, realising that the problem was not solely a military one, expressed an almost unanimous feeling in favour of the establishment of a Republican Government.

The members of the Executive who were able to do so met secretly in Dublin on 25 October, constituted themselves the Republican Government and appointed de Valera as President with a twelve-member Council of State. A Proclamation was issued by the Army Executive on 28th October and it was arranged that documents from the Executive's Defence Department would be signed both by de Valera, as President and Liam Lynch, as Chief-of-Staff. While de Valera recognised the views of Lynch and the Executive, he made his position clear in a letter to Joe McGarrity: "If the Army thinks I am too moderate, well, let them try to get a better President and go ahead."[6]

After the Republican Army Executive meeting, Liam Lynch expressed his satisfaction and optimism in a letter to his brother Tom: "It was a splendid review of the actual situation all over Ireland ... We are absolutely confident that the Free State is beaten and that it is only a matter of time when they must give in ...."[7]

However the Provisional Government were determined "to fight to the bitter end."[8] Since Michael Collins's death W. T. Cosgrave had taken over Chairmanship of the Provisional Government. (He was also President of the Dáil.) On 24 November Erskine Childers, who had been taken prisoner, was executed by order of the Provisional Government. This led to Liam Lynch allegedly issuing an order on 30 November, (which later fell into pro-Treaty hands and was used for propaganda purposes) stating that "all members of the Provisional Parliament who were present and voted for the Murder Bill will be shot at sight."[9]

The Dáil passed the Irish Free State Constitution Bill, and after a year of turmoil the Provisional Government ceased to be and the Irish Free State was officially born on 6 December 1922.

On 7 December, Dáil Deputy Sean Hales was shot dead. (Because he was absent he had not voted on the special emergency powers and controversy has surrounded this shooting.) Deputy Padraig O'Máille, who was travelling in a side-car with him, received a slight bullet wound. Early next morning four Republicans who had been prisoners since the fall of the Four Courts at the end of June (Rory O'Connor, Liam Mellows, Joe McKelvey and Dick Barrett) were taken from their cells in Mountjoy and executed. Their execution order was signed by Richard Mulcahy.[10]

By now the Civil War had taken a cruel and bitter twist. During the closing days of 1922 and the early days of 1923 there were executions and deaths. Fifty-five executions had been carried out by order of the Free State authorities, and more were pending. (The total number of executions during hostilities was seventy-nine.) The Free State began to introduce a policy of sentencing prisoners to death in places where Republican activities were taking place, so the conflict now lacked any human dignity. By this time the guerilla warfare was almost over and the Republicans were reduced to snipings and skirmishes. It was evident that military victory was no longer a possibility for the Republicans, yet doggedly and stubbornly both sides continued the battle.

Liam Deasy, who was captured on 18 January and faced with death, some days later signed an unconditional surrender order. Though Deasy's comrades regarded this action as traitorous at the time, it was later regarded as courageous and just; it saved the lives of many Republican prisoners. Copies of this order were sent by the Free State Government and to the members of the Executive for their signatures. Deasy had already begun to see the futility of continuing the fight, but his companions "outside" and especially Liam Lynch became more determined.

However, by 10 April many Republicans had begun to accept the futility of further resistance. When Liam Lynch and other members of the executive had assembled in Bill Houlihan's house outside Fermoy for a meeting they were surrounded by Free State troops. They tried to escape but Liam Lynch was fatally wounded on the Knockmealdown mountains.

On 26 and 27 April the remaining Republican Army Council members met. With de Valera presiding over the meeting they decided that armed resistance to the Free State forces should be terminated.

De Valera, by this time, felt that a compromise should be made if the Republicans were to work within the frame of constitutional and political realities. Though the Republicans had decided on an unconditional surrender, many were not prepared to hand in their arms and so they still constituted a threat to the Free State. Meanwhile the Free State continued to arrest Republicans, and many of them remained "on the run." Jim Kearney and Timmy Sullivan, both of whom had been in the Béal na mBláth ambush, were among the many who remained in prison. While de Valera was addressing an election meeting in Ennis on 15 August 1923, he himself was arrested, put in jail but headed the poll in Clare.

After a hunger strike by Republican prisoners in most prisons during October and November, the Government began to release people in a "dribble" system. Timmy Sullivan was released in October 1923 and Jimmy Kearney was held until the following February. By then only about 20 prisoners remained in Free State jails.

The results of the 1923 election legitimised the Free State because the newly-formed Cumann na nGaedheal party had 63 candidates elected. Despite the absence in jail of many Sinn Fein candidates the 44 elected showed continued support for the Republicans. It also showed that the Sinn Fein abstentionist principle was no longer popular and so de Valera, on his release from jail in July 1924, set his sights on a method of entering the Dáil.

The task of establishing order and the concern of bringing stability to the twenty-six counties of Ireland now rested with the Cumann na nGaedheal government which held office until 1932.

Appendix 1

John McPeak and the *Slieve Na mBan*

After Michael Collins's funeral John (Jock) McPeak returned from Dublin to Cork and resumed escort duties as gunner in the armoured car, serving with General Emmet Dalton and General Tom Ennis.

Some days later he accompanied a number of soldiers and an intelligence officer on a farmyard raid in Dublin Hill outside Cork city where he witnessed the arrest of two anti-Treatyites who were pushed into a Crossley tender. Standing in front of the tender, McPeak heard sudden bursts of gunfire, rushed to the rear to investigate and found both men bleeding. Sean Donoghue died instantly and his badly injured companion died later. McPeak openly expressed his feelings of revulsion at such a barbaric deed but he only got a rebuff. From that moment on, he was determined to get out of the Free State Army and out of Ireland at the first opportunity.

After a few weeks he was transferred from Victoria Barracks, Cork to the Devonshire Arms Hotel headquarters, Bandon, and went out on duty in West Cork.

During this period the trim six-foot tall McPeak befriended another Scotsman who worked in the mess room, and who was married to a local girl. One evening the three of them went to Gertie Leary's public house in the South Main Street, Bandon, where McPeak was introduced to Anna Mulqueen and May Twomey, members of Cumann na mBan. In conversation, he told them that initially when he was recruited in Scotland, he believed that both "the Free Staters and the Republicans were the same, and fighting for the same cause." (This was prior to the Civil War.)

Basically, he supported the Republican cause, as both his parents had come from Ireland. During the early part of 1921 he was at a meeting with about twenty men in St. Joseph's Hall in Tollcross, Glasgow; the men had obtained arms and had them packed and ready for shipment to Ireland when the hall was raided. All the men, including McPeak, were arrested and sent to Barlinie prison where they were roughly treated. They were released following the signing of the Treaty in December 1921.

When McPeak and his comrades were recruited under the authority of the Provisional Government it was the men's belief that they were being brought to Ireland to join the IRA. McPeak was a welcome recruit, having been a machine-gunner in the British Army (he had served in the machine-gun corps with the Sutherland Highlanders from 1916 to 1919). "We were just told that they wanted soldiers in Ireland."

Shortly after his arrival in Ireland, the Civil War began; McPeak was commissioned as gunner in the *Slieve na mBan* armoured car that escorted Michael Collins on his final journey.

After the incident in the Dublin Hill farmyard, McPeak, appalled by this and other atrocities that were being committed, was determined to get out if possible; he feared that some reaction of his while working within the force would put his own life in danger, so he decided he would desert and hope for the best.

Anna Mulqueen and May Twomey, the Cumann na mBan girls whom he met in Gertie Leary's public house, got in touch with Tadhg Sullivan and Dan Holland. The Republicans subsequently contacted McPeak and agreed to help him desert, but to prove his loyalty he would also have to bring with him the *Slieve na mBan* armoured car. In return they would enable him to return safely to Scotland. Without the armoured car he was of no benefit to the Republicans. Several meetings took place as the two young women liaised with McPeak.

Jim Grey (Cork) was selected by the Republicans to drive the armoured car and was then sent to meet McPeak. Both men agreed that on the evening of 5 October 1922, Grey would be ready to drive the vehicle. That evening Tom Kelleher waited at Tinkers' Cross while Jim Kearney with Pat Dempsey waited at Coolmountain Cross for Grey to flash the lights of the armoured car three times to announce their approach. However they waited in vain; this plan fell through.

Billy Barry, a motor mechanic, was then selected for the job. He came from Cork and stayed at O'Mahony's of Laragh outside Bandon. It was decided that McPeak would inform the women when the armoured car was "out on a run" so that with McPeak's co-operation, the Free State party could be overpowered.

Nevertheless, McPeak hesitated because he feared for the lives of some of the companions whom he had got to know in the pro-Treaty Forces. He suggested an alternative plan.

On the evening of 2 December 1922, May Twomey cycled out from Bandon to Laragh, taking with her a Free State uniform that had been secured by McPeak. She told Billy Barry that the time was right. Barry changed into the uniform, took May Twomey's bicycle and cycled towards Bandon. "I was to meet McPeak and Anna Mulqueen walking out the Dunmanway road. When I saw the couple I stopped and asked if I was on the right road for Bandon."

Immediately Barry recognised the Scottish accent. "Aren't you the gunner in the armoured car?" said Barry.

"Yes," came the response, "McPeak is my name."

Barry then handed over the bicycle to Anna Mulqueen and the two men, both now in Free State uniform, walked into town. They went into the Devonshire Arms Hotel, army headquarters, and upstairs to a room where Sergeant Thomas Cooney, the most recent driver of the armoured car, was playing cards with a few more men. (The crew assigned to the armoured car on this occasion was different from the crew that had been on it during the journey with Michael Collins from Dublin to West Cork in August.)

Lieutenant Peter Gough had issued an order that while the men were in barracks an air-valve should be removed from the engine to immobilise the car, and that McPeak was to hold the lock of the gun.

McPeak entered the room, removed his greatcoat and proceeded to hang it up with the other coats. He quickly searched the pockets of the other coats while Billy Barry remained at the door. One of the men seated at the table shouted, "Mac, would you ever get me some cigarettes?" McPeak gladly obliged.

So McPeak and Barry left, went down town and had a pint. McPeak decided he would say the shops were closed, but that he had cigarettes in his greatcoat pocket.

Back upstairs, while getting out the cigarettes, he transferred the parts for the vehicle to his own greatcoat pocket. He pulled the packet of cigarettes from his coat pocket and deposited them on the table. "I think it's getting cold," he ventured, putting on his coat. "I feel like a walk. Like to come?" he said calmly, to an uneasy Billy Barry.

They went down the stairs and into the yard where there was a number of soldiers. A dance was in progress in the hall upstairs. Thinking quickly, McPeak spoke loudly so that he would be heard, "Let's go to the dance!"

As the two men were going up the stairs to the dance-hall an awkward moment occurred when a Free State officer, who knew Billy Barry, was coming down against them. "Oh hallo!" he said.

"Hallo, sir!" said Barry, saluting him smartly.

Luck was on Barry's side, because on the previous day there had been a slight mutiny in Drimoleague barracks, which resulted in a number of men having been transferred from there to the Devonshire Arms headquarters, and "they were wandering around without guns." Consequently, Billy Barry did not appear out of place. The officer's suspicions were not aroused.

The two men continued as far as the dance-hall door. "This way," said McPeak, who led the way. They mingled with the on-lookers and wove through the room, down a back stairs and into the courtyard. Smartly they walked to the armoured car and set to work. Billy Barry began to check the engine while McPeak was up on the body. When questioned by one of the men, McPeak said he was cleaning the gun. Barry, having inserted the loose piece of equipment, closed the bonnet and jumped into the driver's seat. "I was about to start the engine when I heard the gate closing; an officer came along and posted a sentry in charge of the car. I thought the game had been given away on me. I was a sitting duck!" said Barry. Immediately McPeak spoke, "We're going out on a raid, Sir. There's a driver in the car. You'd better get the gate open for us."

As they were pulling out an officer named John Sullivan realised what their intention was and jumped on the back. McPeak failed to persuade him to get off. So they drove with him up Convent Hill and out the Crookstown road. When Sullivan wouldn't get off for McPeak, he told him he'd shoot him. So Sullivan jumped.

Once the two men passed certain points along the road Republicans helped them. They were hidden behind ditches and began to fell trees (previously partially cut) so that any pursuers would be impeded, and would be compelled to turn back. McPeak and Barry drove towards Newcestown, picked up Charles Foley, and continued towards Crookstown to meet Tom Crofts. Later they were joined by Jamie Moynihan and Tim Farrell. A carpet of straw had to be used to urge the *Slieve na mBan* through some stubble fields. (It was only some months previously that the same car had to be helped along with pro-Treaty greatcoats, as Collins's body was being shouldered over rough fields.)

"We travelled through bogs and bye-roads on to Kealkil to meet Ted O'Sullivan O/C 5th brigade. The great weight of the armoured car caused it to sink several times. We had to get planks to dig her out when we travelled along Coolmountain bog-road. For two days we travelled without sleep, and drove at night without the head lights. I was young at the time, but still I felt worn," said Barry.

The men were billeted in a house near Kealkil. Following a

substantial meal, they went to bed. A few hours later they were awakened from a deep sleep and told they were to drive to Ballyvourney and be prepared to attack it. "We couldn't wake McPeak," said Billy Barry, "so we left him. In any case we knew Mick Sullivan of Kilnamartyra would man the gun." While McPeak was certainly tired he was only pretending to be in "a dead sleep." He was now a reluctant machine-gunner. He did not want to attack the men he had left behind just a few days previously.

Billy Barry, Jamie Moynihan, Foley and a few more men drove all night through Ballingeary to attack Ballyvourney. "We arrived at 8 o'clock in the morning and attacked the village, which had been held by Free State soldiers." Mick Sullivan manned the gun of the *Slieve na mBan*, while Billy Barry was in the driver's seat. Jerry Kennedy from over the Kerry boarder commanded a section of men from Kerry in support of the Cork men during this attack. "It wasn't long," said Barry, "until the village was ours. We took 125 Staters as prisoners and they captured Tom Kelleher. We told them we'd shoot the lot of the prisoners we held if they didn't let Kelleher free. It didn't take them long to change their minds."

Because the Republicans had no accommodation for the prisoners, they stripped them of their guns, uniforms and boots "and sent them packing into Killarney," making them take their wounded with them. "We got an amount of ammunition plus another armoured car."

All the tyres of the *Slieve na mBan* had been punctured, so it was half-driven and half-pushed back to a farmyard near Guagane Barra. The Republicans removed the turret and gun section, took it away and buried it elsewhere. They also removed some parts from the engine, pushed the car into a shed and covered it with furze.

Over the months ahead the Republicans tried unsuccessfully to get tyres for the car. In the end it remained beneath the furze for a number of years. The Free State soldiers were looking for the *Slieve na mBan* until December 1931. Then they found it while combing the area.

So the *Slieve na mBan* was towed away to the Curragh

minus gun and turret. Though the car has been preserved and is held in the Curragh Army Training Headquarters, the original gun which was used by Jock McPeak on the day Michael Collins was shot, has never been located. Contrary to the general opinion, it is a replacement gun and turret that is now mounted on the *Slieve na mBan*.

Meanwhile, back in Kealkil, Jock McPeak rose to eat a hearty breakfast/lunch, and then wandered into the farmyard to discover that the *Slieve na mBan* armoured car was gone. He was informed that his companions of the night before had taken it on a raid. That December evening McPeak was told he was going on a further journey; exhausted, he arrived at "a safe house" in Kilgarvan, Co. Kerry. After a meal he went straight to bed. At daybreak he was abruptly awakened, and told that Free State soldiers were raiding the area. He pulled on his trousers, grabbed his coat and boots and ran downstairs. Through the window he saw that the street was thronged with soldiers.

Calmly, the householder led McPeak out to a turf loft at the rear of the house, and showed him a concealed attic opening. When McPeak had ascended the ladder, the man removed it. McPeak had a tense moment when the soldiers flashed up the lights; he held his breath and remained until he got the "all clear."

Just as he sat down to breakfast again he heard a sudden burst of gunfire. He bolted to the back door, ran across the yard and over the wall; he waded through a river and up a few fields at the back. He picked his way carefully towards cover and encountered some more Republicans who were also evading capture.

McPeak had only had two meals since he left the security of Bandon Barracks a few days previously. As the days progressed he had to move further into the Kerry hills, and as he did so, the danger of being captured lessened. Over the cold winter months of December 1922 and January 1923, in rain, hail and snow, he learned what it was like to live "on the run".

However, he had a break on Christmas night when he was taken to Ballingeary where Republicans had organised a party. "It was a lively night with singing, dancing, and plenty to eat and drink."

A few weeks later a comrade introduced him to five men who had also deserted from the Free State army, and who lived in a derelict cottage in the Kerry mountains, but this companionable interlude was short-lived. Soon he had to move on and keep moving as the troops had begun to scour the hills.

As the months progressed and the spring days lengthened, he was taken in by Dan Kelleher; here he lived and worked for some weeks on the Kelleher farm, hidden in the Kerry hills. Now he relished the home-made brown bread, bacon and cabbage and all "the other satisfying country cooking" given to him by Mrs Kelleher after his day's work.

Once more word came that his life was in danger, so again he went "on the run." As the pressure increased, he wondered and asked how he could get out of the country. By this time he desperately wanted to get out.

By early June, arrangements were being made for his trip across the Irish Sea. He was escorted one morning to the home of John Sullivan and family, where he stayed for a few days. Dressed in a Republican-supplied new suit of clothes, he prepared for his journey to Scotland.

When the car came to collect him, there was a priest at the wheel (or a man dressed as a priest, McPeak couldn't be sure) and two women, one in the back with McPeak and another in the passenger seat. The four set out for Cork city. Free State soldiers saluted the "priest" as they passed through many towns and villages. The large bouquet of flowers, held by McPeak's supposed partner in the back seat, shielded his face from view when they were stopped in Blarney.

On the night of 14 June 1923, McPeak stayed in Cork with IRA sympathisers. The following morning he was escorted to a cattle boat which was sailing to Glasgow that evening. Some members of the crew collaborated. They gave him food on this rather tense journey, and smuggled him ashore just outside his native city.

Fearing arrest, Jock McPeak did not return to his home in Parkhead; instead he lodged in cheap boarding houses. However, his freedom was short-lived. On 2 July, he was taken in for questioning by the Glasgow police. Shortly afterwards the Dublin Metropolitan Police arrived from Dublin and escorted him to Cork where he was jailed in the military barracks.

Because there were no extradition laws covering the new Free State, John Robertson, a local MP, asked in the House of Commons by what authority McPeak had been deported. The Solicitor-General for Scotland responded by saying that Irish warrants could be endorsed in Scotland under the procedure regulated by statutory provisions.

Back in Cork, McPeak was charged by the military authorities with having deserted from the army. He was remanded in custody for ten days. But McPeak had deserted from the Provisional Government forces and had taken the armoured car on 2 December, 1922. The Free State did not come into existence *de facto*, until 6 December, 1922. So McPeak had deserted from a division of the Irish Army, but was arrested and handed over to the Free State Army authorities. Furthermore he was a Scottish national and had been arrested without a warrant. When his case came up for trial, the military authorities refused to let the prosecution witnesses testify. His offence of desertion was committed under the jurisdiction of a body which militarily no longer existed. He was discharged.

But as he walked down the steps of the Courthouse in Cork he was re-arrested by the civil authorities, and returned to Cork jail. This time he was charged with the stealing of the Rolls-Royce armoured car, taken from Government forces in Bandon on 2 December 1922. The car and its contents were valued at "£1,000 and upwards."

John McPeak's brother, Frank, came to Dublin to arrange legal aid, and got Mr Comyn, KC, a prominent lawyer in Dublin to handle the case. Frank, who had served in the Royal Navy during the war, booked into a guesthouse for the night.

During the night he was awakened by police, arrested, and conveyed to military barracks. He was charged with aiding in the acquisition and the exportation from Scotland of arms and ammunition "for the Irregulars to be used against the Free State." However, despite an affidavit by General O'Sullivan that Frank McPeak had conspired to acquire the armaments, he was released due to "insufficient evidence" and he returned to Scotland.

John McPeak believed that he faced execution. This belief was shared by the Republicans who had helped to get him to Scotland. Back in West Cork a rescue attempt was being planned. They looked at several different angles. Five men were ready "to jump him from custody" during his court appearance and a full plan had been structured. However, because of the risk to their men, Liam Deasy and Dan Holland decided it would be suicidal, so the plan was abandoned.

John McPeak eventually went on trial before District Justice O'Sullivan. Captain J. Healy, State Solicitor for West Cork, prosecuted. W. D. Moiller, Solicitor appeared for the defence. The evidence disclosed that the parts removed from the armoured car to immobilise it had been secured by McPeak with an accomplice. These had been reinserted, and the car had been taken from the barracks' yard without permission.

McPeak was the only member missing from the Devonshire Arms headquarters when the loss of the car was reported by John Sullivan (who had returned after being pushed off the car at Convent Hill). A search party had been sent "to pursue the car," but six miles out, the road had been blocked "by felled trees."

During McPeak's trial there was no mention of the shooting of Michael Collins. He pleaded guilty to taking the armoured car for his own protection; for this he received a sentence of six years imprisonment, and was sent to serve his time in Portlaoise prison. During his stay there, he participated in a hunger strike in sympathy with Republican prisoners. During one Sunday Mass a pastoral letter was read condemning Republican prisoners for their activities. The men left the prison chapel during the reading of the letter, and as a punishment were confined to a diet of bread and water. A hunger strike followed. However, like many of the men McPeak abandoned the hunger strike when he became weak. Eventually the protest was called off.

In July 1928, John McPeak was released from Portlaoise prison having served five of his six years. Penniless, he returned home to Glasgow. Free, but insecure, he decided to use a pseudonym to aid him while seeking employment. Various temporary jobs came his way; he worked as truck driver, crane driver, furniture remover, until finally, because of his unsettled state, he decided to move south to England.

A job with a construction company south of London brought him security. He worked driving a crane with this company during the building of the present Bank of England and he was accustomed to go out with his pals to a local dance hall. One night he met an English girl of Irish descent. In June 1932 they were married. Two children, a boy and a girl, were born to them.

He changed his name by deed poll and lived the rest of his life under the assumed name. He died in 1974 and his wife died a few years later.

Appendix II

Letter from the Provisional Government at 8.40 p.m on 14-7-1922

General Michael Collins

You have been entrusted with supreme command of the National Army and with General Mulcahy and General O'Duffy you have been constituted a War Council to direct the military operations now in progress. The Government's action is dictated by a determination that the splendid valour and devotion of the Army shall be inspired and directed to yield its full fruit for the Salvation of the Nation.

The Government recognises itself as the servant of the IRISH People, and as such its duty is to see that the expressed will of the Irish people shall be carried into effect. An armed minority, possessing no authority, is waging war against the people to force them to submit to a dictatorship; and the army which so recently freed the people from a foreign tyranny must now resist this domestic encroachment upon their liberties.

The Irish Army, therefore, is fighting for the same principle as that for which we fought the British, the right of the Irish people to be masters in their own country, to decide for themselves the way in which they shall live, and the system by which they shall be governed. For that principle they have made, and are prepared to make further sacrifices. Many have died, many have been wounded. They have died and are suffering that the people of Ireland may be free.

The "irregulars'" method of warfare is utterly destructive of the economic life of the nation. Sheer brigandage is a fair term to apply to it. Wherever they go, they burn and wreck property; destroy roads, railways, and bridges; seize food, clothing and supplies even from the poorest people; conscript men into their ranks; and use forced labour. In short they are doing their best to ruin and demoralise their country.

From these outrages the Government and the Army will protect the people. The fight is for the revival of the Nation; for the free expression and effective execution of the people's will; for internal peace and order—in other words for the establishment of all the signs by which a nation is to be held worthy of consideration among the states of the world.

Arthur Griffith

Michael McDonnchada
Acting Secretary to the Provisional Government.

(Signed by):
K. O'Higgins   L.T. MacCosgair
P.J. Hogan   J. McGrath

Appendix III

Military Censorship
General Instructions—July 1922

1. The Army must always be referred to as the "Irish Army," "The National Army," "National Forces," "National Troops" or simply "The Troops."

2. The Irregulars must not be referred to as "Executive Forces:" nor described as "Forces:" or "Troops." They are to be called "Bands" or "Bodies" or "Armed men" or "Irregulars."

3. Irregular leaders are not to be referred to as of any rank such as "Commandant" etc. and are not to be called Officers.

4. No news of movements of the troops may be published.

5. No news may be published with regard to the movements of newly-enrolled members of the Army, movements of food ships or trains, or transport of arms or equipment for Army purposes.

6. Descriptions of a military operation must not be published while the operation is still uncompleted, as for instance, an encirclement movement.

7. Articles or letters as to the treatment of Irregular prisoners may not be published.

8. The Censors are not to insert the words of their own in any article submitted to them. Their business is to conceal what is objected to. They may however propose to substitute

words or phrases, such as "Irregular" for "Republicans," "fired at" for "attacked," "seized" for "commandeered" or "kidnapped by Irregulars" for "averted," "enrolled" for "enlisted."

9. Letters, news or articles dealing with proposals for peace or negotiations with the Irregulars should not be passed without first submitting them to the Chief Censor.

Appendix IV

Peace proposals—19th August, 1922

The following terms have been communicated to Major General Dalton by a Committee of prominent citizens of Cork, and after consultation with his staff he has agreed to communicate them to General Michael Collins.

1 A week's truce is to be immediately arranged on the basis of the existing military position.

2 During this interval facilities are to be afforded to the Republican Military and Political leaders to hold a meeting to discuss the making of peace on the following basis:-

   1 Republican opposition to the Government and Parliament is to be on constitutional lines.

   2 Members of the Republican Forces who desire to return to civil life will be allowed to return to their occupations without molestation or penalisation.

   3 Members of the Republican Forces who wish to join the National Army will be received therein with due recognition of rank and service.

   4 Arms and amunitions in possession of the Republican Forces will be handed over to a Committee to be mutually agreed upon.

   5 There will be a general amnesty of all Political prisoners.

Collins's Response

On Saturday night Collins wrote a message which was to be wired to General Dalton the following day:

Wireless despatch received. Will you say by cipher who the prominent citizens responsible for the offer are?

Have the Irregular leaders, political and military, agreed to the offer and is it made on their behalf?

Government offer published in the Press 5th June, and conveyed to the People's Rights Association, Cork stands. For our guidance the terms of this are:-

First:- Transfer into the National Armoury of all war materials.

Second:- Restoration, without exception, of all seized property and money.

Third:- Particulars be furnished, bridges, roads, railways which are or have been mined or rendered otherwise unsafe.

Appendix V

W/T Office Portobello—16 August 1922

The following messages from Cork and Limerick have been intercepted here at 9.15.

Gen. O'Duffy to Gen. Dalton: What is your position?

Gen. Dalton to Gen. O'Duffy: All quiet on all fronts. I occupy Cork City, Queenstown, Fermoy, Rosscarbery; have moved on Macroom and Mitchelstown: believe O'Connell at Mitchelstown will write. Have you Mallow or will I take it?

Gen, O'Duffy to Gen. Dalton: Advancing south, expect to be at Blackwater from Waterford to Kerry by week-end, attack on Mallow proceeding now. Did Limerick ship arrive with 250 men?

Gen, Dalton to Gen. O'Duffy: —Ship has returned to Limerick, ship arrived. I will attack Mallow from Fermoy.

Gen. O'Duffy to Gen. Dalton: I am moving on Macroom from west tomorrow.

Gen. Dalton to Gen. O'Duffy: I bet you £5 I will be there before you.

Gen. O'Duffy to Gen. Dalton: Good man, accepted.

Ends
Mulcahy Papers P7/B/70/80

Notes

List of Abbreviations
    P.G. – Provisional Government
    C.in.C – Commander-In-Chief
    M.P. – Mulcahy Papers
    P.R.O. – Public Record Office
    D/I – Director of Intelligence
    Q.M.G.– Quarter Master General

Introduction

Part I

1 The Irish Republican Brotherhood (IRB) was founded in Dublin on 17 March, 1858 by James Stephens—with John O'Mahony providing funds from New York. As Head-Centre, Stephens designed the organisation along secret lines. It lost force for some time but was reorganised in 1873. The Easter Rising of 1916 was planned by a small group of the Military Council. Following the collapse of the Rising, the IRB was reorganised under Michael Collins and after Thomas Ashe's death Collins replaced him as secretary. The Supreme Council favoured the Treaty, so the IRB split during the Civil War. Collins was in the organisation until his death.

2 Sam Maguire, b.1879 Dunmanway; worked as a clerk in London General Post Office; became a supporter of the IRB, GAA and Irish Volunteers, and was a close friend of Collins. He was Chief Intelligence Officer for the Volunteers in London and supplied arms to Collins for

the Irish cause. Being a keen sportsman he captained the London teams that played in All-Ireland football finals in 1903, 1905, 1906. As a memorial to his GAA work the "Sam Maguire Cup" was presented in perpetuity.

3 Michael O'Brien interview with author, 15/6/1974.

4 Elizabeth Countess of Fingall, *Seventy Years Young*, p. 409.

5 *Ibid.*

6 Public Records Office, Dublin.

7 National Library, Dublin MS 13329.

8 Executed leaders:- 3 May: Padraic Pearse, Thomas J. Clarke and Thomas MacDonagh. 4 May: Joseph Plunkett, Edward Daly, William Pearse and Michael O' Hanrahan. 5 May: John MacBride. 8 May: Eamonn Ceannt, Michael Mallin, Con Colbert and Sean Heuston. 9 May: Thomas Kent. 12 May: James Connolly and Sean Mac Diarmada.

9 May 1, 1916, entered as "Collins M. 16 Rathdown Road, North Circular Rd, Irish Prisoner 48F."

10 Thomas Ashe, b. Kinard, near Dingle, Co. Kerry; active in Gaelic League and Irish Volunteers; for his part in the 1916 Rising in Ashbourne he was sentenced to life imprisonment; released June 1917, became active in Sinn Fein and Volunteers, arrested in August, sentenced to two years imprisonment. He went on hunger strike for political status but failed to achieve his goal. On 25 September 1917 he died while being forcibly fed. Collins delivered the oration at his graveside.

11 According to the IRB constitution, the President, in fact, as well as by right, was regarded as head of the Government of the Irish Republic. However, the constitution of the IRB had subsequently to be amended

to take into account an oath required by Dail deputies and officials committing them to support and defend the Irish Republic and its government.

12 Dave Neligan interview with author, 30/1/1974. Neligan, one of the G-men in The Castle, later one of the British Secret Service acting as agent for Collins.

13 This episode happened with the knowledge and approval of the Minister of Defence, Cathal Brugha. (Eleven British Intelligence men were shot dead and four were wounded, two Auxiliaries who intervened were killed and another uninvolved officer was also killed.) Collins said afterwards (in London) to Birkenhead, "Our lads would have been wiped out. We got there first." 26 Oct. 1922.

14 Member of the Hales family from Knocknacurra. Donal Hales was involved with the organisation of a ship load of arms to Ireland. Collins supplied him with material on the Irish situation for his newspaper reporting.

15 Letter to Liam Lynch, 16 May 1921.

16 Another member of the Hales family from Knocknacurra. During the War of Independence and the Civil War, Madge Hales (Murphy) communicated dispatches between the Third West Cork Brigade and GHQ. She was the personal link between Collins and her brother Donal Hales in Italy in connection with the arms shipment.

17 Ulick O'Connor, *Oliver St. John Gogarty*, p. 193.

18 Madge Hales interview with author, 20/6/1971.

19 Tom Barry interview with author, 17/3/1976.

20 Leon O'Broin, *Michael Collins*, p.85—Frank Thornton memoirs.

21 T. Ryle Dwyer, *Michael Collins and the Treaty*, p. 46.

22 *Ibid.* p 48. Also Piaras Beaslai, *Michael Collins and The Making of a New Ireland*, p. 275.

23 T. Ryle Dwyer, *Michael Collins and the Treaty.* p 46.

24 Emmet Dalton interview with author 3/10/1973.

25 Frank Pakenham, *Peace By Ordeal*, p. 239.

26 Sir John Lavery, *The Life of a Painter*, p. 214.

27 Haden Talbot, *Michael Collins' Own Story*, p. 144 to 151. See also T. Ryle Dwyer, *Michael Collins and the Treaty*, p. 44 to 53.

28 Collins to O'Kane, *Freeman's Journal*, 6 Dec. 1921.

29 Sir John Lavery, *The Life of a Painter*, p. 214.

30 Rex Taylor, *Michael Collins*, p. 124. Letter John O'Kane to Taylor.

31 Fifty-seven opposed the Treaty, sixty-four were for the Treaty.

32 See M. Ryan, *The Real Chief*, pp.106 to 111.

33 Sean MacBride interview with author 23/10/1978.

Part II

1 Margery Forester, *Michael Collins: The Lost Leader*, p. 317.

2 Calton Younger, *A State of Disunion*, p. 154.

3 Ernest Blythe to author 25/10/1973. Collins was in Cork when word of Wilson's assassination reached him.

4 Ernest Blythe interview with author 25/10/1973.

5 Lloyd George to Collins, 22 June 1922. M.P. P7/B/244/1. See also Sheila Lawlor, *Britain and Ireland* 1914-23, p. 191.

6 Ernest Blythe interview with author 8/11/1973.

7 Reginald Dunne and Joseph O'Sullivan were hanged at Wandsworth prison, London, on 10 August 1922.

8 Collins to Cosgrave, 6 August 1922, M.P. P7/B/29/62.

9 Cosgrave to Collins, 7 August 1922, M. P. P7/B/29/50.

10 Ulick O'Connor, *The Sunday Independent*, November 2nd, 1980 reviewing *Michael Collins*, by Leon O'Broin.

11 Emmet Dalton interview with author 2/3/1974.

12 Lloyd George to Collins, 22 June 1922, M.P. P7/B/244/1 & 2.

13 Sir Nevil Macready, *Annals of an Active Life*, Vol 2 pp. 652, 653.

14 Provisional Government minutes, P.G. meeting 27 June 1922, M.P. P7/B/244/7.

15 Ernest Blythe interview with author 20/3/1974.

16 *Ibid.*

17 Provisional Government minutes, P.G. meeting 2 July 1922, M.P. P7/B/244/23, P7/B/244/26 & 27.

18 P.Gov. minutes, P.G. meeting 13 July 1922, M.P. P7/B/ 244/30. By 17 July, the number of men in the Army reached 15,000 approx. Later, further authority was given by the Government to increase the army strength to 35,000.

19 Collins to Griffith—memo on establishment of War Council, 12 July, M. P. P7/B/177—quoted Hopkinson, *Green Against Green*, p.136.

20 P. Gov. minutes, meeting (morning) 12 July 1922. M.P. P7/B/244/58; also P.R.O. P.G. 57. 12 July 1922.

21 P.G. minutes, meeting (evening) 12 July 1922. M.P. P7/ B/244/61. *Ibid.*

22 Collins's notebook, 12 July 1922—abbreviated version

of these appointments.

23 Collins—General Instructions, July 1922. M.P. P7/B/52/5.

24 Report from Capt. Stapleton, Observer and Capt. Russell, Pilot, to Collins, 17 July 1922, M.P. P7/B/107/69.

25 Collins's handwritten notes, 14 July 1922, M.P. P7/B/18/29 & P7/B/18/27 & P7/B/18/28. M.P. (Collins's notes: "Immediate Objective—To prepare for an attack on Waterford at once—to have Carrick-On-Suir in mind for occupying almost immediately after" He commanded Gen. Prout to "Supply a gun team to report of Gen. O'Duffy". Collins wanted men to move on Kilkenny, Thurles, Castlecomer, and distribution of men and arms. 14 July 1922.)

26 Collins's note book, p. 14 & 15, 14 July 1922, M.P. P7/B/43/13.

27 Collins to Chief of General Staff, 14 July 1922, M.P. P7/B/49/50.

28 Collins to Lieut Gen. O'Connell, 14 July 1922, M.P. P7/B/17/49 & P7/B/17/50.

29 Collins to Quarter Master General 16 July 1922. Ibid; Q.M.G. to Collins (list) 15 July, 1922. M.P. P7/B/3/147; compiled 17 July 1922, M.P. P7/B/3/145.

30 Collins to Quarter Master General 17 July 1922, M.P. P7/B/3/143.

31 Provisional Government minutes, meeting 12 July 1922, M.P. P7/B/244/58,

32 Provisional Government letter to Collins signed by A. Griffith, Michael McDonnchada, K. O'Higgins, P.J. Hogan, L.T. MacCosgair, J. McGrath. (Handwritten on top: "original sent to Gen. Collins, 8.40 p.m. today 14-7-

'22.") M.P. P7/B/29/233 and P7/B/29/234 also 235. See Appendix II.

33 *Irish Times*, 19 July 1922.

34 Collins's notebook, 13 Aug 1922. That night he wrote in his notebook: "First day at P'Bello. Staff meeting at 4 o'c. Spent morning rather wastefully owing to delay B. of Works in fitting up rooms for working in."

35 Collins wrote to Acting Chairman (Cosgrave) and signed himself Chairman, 31 July 1922,—re British Gov. Stocks kept in Bank of I. in Belfast. M.P. P7/B/29/143; Collins wrote to Acting Chairman and signed himself Chairman, 31 July, 1922,—re prisoners on hunger strike in Derry jail, M.P. P7/B/29/131; also 31 July 1922. M.P. P7/B/29/133: Collins wrote to Churchill under the heading of Chairman's Office—re Diseases of Animals Act, 27 July 1922, Blythe Papers p. 27/65.

36 There are notes written at 12 midnight, e.g. 17 Aug. 1922, M.P. P7/B/2/83.

37 Collins to Churchill. 15 July 1922 P.R.O. CO 38573. (Churchill's letter to Collins P. G. minutes, meeting 8 July 1922. M.P. P7/B/244/48.

38 Collins to Churchill 25 July 1922, P.R.O. CO 38573.

39 Cosgrave to Collins 25 July 1922, M.P. P7/B/29/184.

40 Chairman Legion of Irish Ex-Servicemen to Collins, 25 July 1922, M.P. P7/B/9/63. "100 Artillery men, 100 Drivers, 100 Machine gunners, 100 Engineers, 100 Signallers" (20 Instructors were selected for the Curragh.) M.P. P7/B/9/52.

41 Collins's memo—General Situation—26 July 1922, M.P. P7/B/28/45 & 46.

42 Collins's memo, 26 July 1922, M.P. P7/B/28/60, *Ibid.*

43 Collins to Cosgrave—re bank raids, 9 Aug. 1922, M.P.

P7/B/29/44; Cosgrave to Collins—position of southern banks, 18 July 1922; Collins to Cosgrave, 28 July 1922, M.P. P7a/50.

44 Margery Forester, *Michael Collins: The Lost Leader*, p. 329.

45 Collins to Director of Intelligence, 31 July 1922, M.P. P7/B/4/90.

46 Collins to Director of Intelligence 3 August 1922, M.P. P7/B/4/74,

47 Collins to Acting Major General Tobin, 20 July 1922, M.P. P7/B/4/123.

48 Cosgrave to Collins—re purchase in England of "arms by the Irregulars" 29 July 1922, 30 July—correspondence of information received from Cope, M.P. P7/B/29/149, P7/B/29/150 also 151 and 152; D/I to Collins, 5 Aug. 1922: "Mr Childers made an attempt to get away to USA on the Carmenia from here yesterday ... "— M.P. P7/B/4/56; 7 Aug. 1922. Collins to D/I suggested, "The idea that would be most suitable would be that he should be arrested as a stow-away."—M.P. P7/B/4/54.

49 Emmet Dalton interview with author, 2/4/1974.

50 Collins to Acting Chairman,—Interim Report—5 Aug. 1922, M.P. P7/B/29/87 to P7/B/29/100.

51 Dr. Gerald Ahern interview with author 10/8/1974. His brother Dr. Leo was medical doctor with Provisional Government forces in Portobello Barracks, Dublin. Later he took over Shanakiel Hospital for the forces.
    Dr. Gerald Ahern (D.J.Ahern) was a young qualified doctor who lived near Shanakiel Hospital, where he worked. At the time, he sailed a yacht called *The Gull*, a twelve ton boat, owned by H.P.F. Donegan, Solicitor. Early in August 1922, Harry Donegan approached Dr. Gerard and asked him to take a woman to Rosslare:

"We left on a Friday, and as the wind was against us we were unable to get to Rosslare, but after five days we pulled in at Kilmore Quay. As Waterford was in Government hands, it was easier to arrange transport from there to Dublin. Donegan got a taxi to Rosslare and from there it was arranged that Mary Collins-Powell would travel by train to Dublin. She had details of arrangements about the landing in Cork, and was to inform her brother, Michael Collins, that there were up to 500 men ready to join him in Cork but were lying low due to lack of arms. Also she was in touch with neutral men in the county who would be intermediaries in future talks which might arise, between Michael Collins and leaders of the opposing forces."

While Mary Collins-Powell travelled to Dublin, Dr. Gerald with Harry Donegan and Fr. Donal Murphy O'Connor returned to Crosshaven with *The Gull* and upon arrival were arrested by anti-Treaty men. They were locked in a shed with armed men on guard. Some days later when the pro-Treaty forces took Cork their guards abandoned them.

52 Collins to Cosgrave, 5 August 1922, M.P. P7/B/29/87 to P7/B/29/100.

53 Dalton to Collins, 10 August 1922, M.P. P7a/50—S.M.

54 *Ibid*, 11 August 1922, M.P. P7a/50.

Chapter 1

1 Arthur Griffith (1871—1922) joined the Irish Volunteers in 1913, took part in the Howth gun-running in July 1914. He was arrested and spent a term in jail. Having led the Irish team in the Treaty negotiations, he later signed and defended it. Later he was elected President of the Dáil. During the Civil War he died of cerebral haemorrhage on 12 August 1922.

2 D.V. Horgan interview with author 14/4/1982. (One of the body-guards to Michael Collins.)

3 *Ibid.*

4 Pat Murray interview with author 23/3/1974.

Chapter 2

1 P.G. meeting 12 July 1922, M.P. P7/B/244/58.

2 Collins's personal notebook 13/7/1922, M.P. P7/B/52/5.

3 Collins's memo, *Organization at G.H.Q.* 19 July 1922, M.P. P7/B/41/88.

4 Collins—*General Routine Orders*, 14 July 1922, M.P. P7a/50.

5 On one occasion Lord Birkenhead and Michael Collins were guests at lunch in the home of Sir John and Lady Hazel Lavery. During the meal Hazel's small Peke dog was pawing at Lord Birkenhead under the table. Hazel realised this, and called the little dog. "Oh, I'm sorry. I thought you were making advances," said Lord Birkenhead.
   Fuming, Collins jumped up, "D'ye mean to insult her?"
   Hazel wishing to calm the situation said, "Lord Birkenhead was only joking."
   "I don't understand such jokes," shouted an irate Collins.

6 Collins, *General Intructions*, July, 1922.
   M.P. P/7/B/52/5.

7 *The Path of Freedom*, by Michael Collins p. 99.

8 Collins's notes, M. P. p. 7/29/3 to 19.

9 Michael Hayes, *The Capuchin Annual*, 1972, p. 279.

10 Affidavit of Thomas A. Kelly, Sligo, 26/9/1967—Private papers held by Dr. Ned Barrett.

11 Ernest Blythe interview with author 19/1/1974.

12 Collins's notebook, Sat. 12 Aug. 1922, M.P. P7a/50.

13 C. in C. (Commander-In-Chief) wire To Confidence, 14 Aug. 1922, M.P. P7/B/70/98.

14 *Ibid*. Handed in 1.20, 15 Aug. 1922, M.P. P7/B/70/82.

15 Chief Of General Staff wire to C. in C. 20 Aug. 1922, M.P. P7/B/70/57.

16 Collins to O'Duffy, 15 Aug. 1922, M.P. P7/B/21/12 & P7/B/21/13 & P7/B/21/14.

17 *Ibid*. 16 Aug. 1922, M.P. P7/B/39/42, Ibid.

18 Collins to Q.M.G. 17 Aug. 1922, (a long angry letter) M.P. P7/B/3/42.

19 Piaras Beaslai, *Michael Collins and The Making of a New Ireland*, Vol.11 p. 424.

20 *The Irish Independent*, 16 August, 1922.

21 Chief Of General Staff wire to Collins 15 Aug. 1922, op. cit. M.P. P7/B/70/89 also P7/B/70/88, P7/B/70/108.

22 Newspaper cutting, 16 Aug. 1922, M.P. P7/B/70/74.

23 Report aerial reconnaissance, 13 Aug. 1922, M.P. P7/B/ 39/21.

24 Personal notes written by Collins, 16 Aug. 1922, M.P. P7a/62.

25 *Ibid*.

26 D.V. Horgan interview with author 23/5/1979.

27 Collins 16 August 1922, M.P. P7/B/28/97.

28 Margery Forester, *Michael Collins: The Lost Leader*,
    p. 331.

29 Collins to Director of Munitions, 19 Aug. 1922, M.P. P7/
    B/4/11; Collins to Director of Purchases, 19 Aug. 1922,
    M.P. P7/B/12/1; *Ibid* Director of Publicity, 19 Aug. 1922,
    M.P. P7/B/14/1; *Ibid.* Prout Southern Division 19 Aug.
    1922, M.P. P7/B/14/1.

30 Personal notes written by Collins, 16 Aug. 1922, M.P.
    P7a/62.

31 O'Duffy to Collins, 12 Aug. 1922. M.P. P7/B/39/32 &
    P7/B/39/33.

32 Collins's notes undated. M.P. P7/B/28/1 & P7/B/28/2.

33 Commander-in-Chief to Officer Commanding S.W.
    Command, 17 Aug. 1922, M.P. P7/B/21/8.

34 Dalton wire to Collins, 19 Aug. 1922, M.P. P7/B/70/62.

35 Ibid. P7/B/70/63 & P7/B/70/65.

36 Commander-In-Chief to Dalton, 19 Aug. 1922, M.P. P7/
    B/20/2. (This was received in Cork by Major General
    Dalton on 19, August, 1922 at 10.50 am.) See Appendix
    IV.

37 Collins's notes, undated, M.P. P7/B/28/1.

38 Elizabeth, Countess of Fingall, *Seventy Years Young*, p.
    403.

39 Piaras Beaslai, *Michael Collins*, p. 427.

40 Margery Forester, *Michael Collins: The Lost Leader*, p.
    333.

41 Collins's notes, 19 Aug. 1922, M.P. P7a/62.

42 Collins to Director of Munitions, 19 Aug. 1922, M.P. P7/
    B/4/11.

43 Collins to Director of Purchases, 19 Aug. 1922, M.P. P7/B/12/1.

44 Collins to Director of Publicity, 19 Aug. 1922, M.P. P7/B/14/1.

45 Collins to Director of Recruiting, 19 Aug. 1922, M.P. P7/B/8/15.

46 Collins to Dalton, 19 Aug. 1922, M.P. P7/B/20/1; Collins to Gen. Price, 19 Aug. 1922 P7/B/3/20/10.

47 Collins to Director of Munitions, 19 Aug. 1922, M.P. P7/B/4/11.

48 Sir John Lavery, *The Life of a Painter*, p. 216.

49 Elizabeth, Countess of Fingall, *Seventy Years Young*, p. 409.

50 Sir John Lavery, *The Life of a Painter*, p 218.

51 *Ibid*, p. 216.

52 *ibid.*, p 216.

53 Frank O'Connor, *The Big Fellow*, p. 211.

Chapter 3

1 Fionán Lynch to Bill Stapelton, 1950. Stapelton interview with author 8/5/1977; also Fionán Lynch in RTE interview.

2 *Ibid.*

3 Collins's notes, Sun. 20 Aug. 1922, M.P. P7a/62.

4 *Ibid.*

5 Frank O'Connor, *The Big Fellow*, p. 211.

6 Collins's notes—diary, 20 Aug. 1922, M.P. P7a/62.

7 Hales was in the south at this time with John L.

O'Sullivan and a complement of men. They had landed at Bantry and taken towns along the West Cork coast.

8 Collins's notes—diary. 20 Aug. 1922, M.P. P7a/62,

9 Fionán Lynch to Bill Stapelton, 1950. Stapelton interview with author 8/5/1977; also Fionán Lynch in RTE interview.

10 *Ibid.*

11 Collins's personal notebook, 20 Aug. 1922, now held by Collins's nephew, Michael Collins.

12 O'Duffy always signed himself as Owen O'Duffy, but the Irish term Eoin is used in many writings.

13 Commander in Chief wire To Confidence, 20 Aug. 1922, M.P. P7/B/70/55.

14 Collins's personal notebook, 20 Aug. 1922.

15 Ibid. He asked that new form should "be here early Tuesday."

16 Notes in Collins's personal notebook—"Army men at Patrickswell depot be moved to the local school and overbridge made traffic-worthy; Lieutenant Drumm in Adare to consolidate his men into one position; trees that blocked road near Croom to be removed; Sergeant Lambert to consolidate all his men in the police barracks while a party of local volunteers under Lieutenant Kerley were to join forces with Commandant Keane's section."

17 John C. Byrne's notes—copy of Collins's diary. Telephone conversation with author 14/8/1978.

18 Ernest Blythe interview with author 9/1/1974.

19 Michael Brennan interview with author 29/11/1973.

20 Commander-In-Chief wire To Confidence, sent 9 p.m. Recd. Portobello 9.40, 20 Aug. 1922, M.P. P7/B/70/54.

21 Commander in Chief wire To Confidence, 20 Aug. 1922, M.P. P7/B/70/55.

22 Collins to P. Gov. encl. "extract from General O'Duffy despatch," 28 July, 1922, M.P. P7/B/38/5.

23 Collins's notes, M.P. P7/B/70/50.

24 C. in C. cypher 4.10 p.m. Limerick. Recd. Portobello, 6.15 p.m. 21 Aug. 1922, M.P. P7/B/70/53.

25 Collins's personal notebook, 20 Aug. 1922, held by Collins's nephew, Michael Collins; See also M.P. 20 Aug. 1922, P7a/62.

26 This is in accordance with time details in Collins's notebook, 20 Aug. 1922.

27 On his return journey the following day he was ambushed at Killarney, again between Castleisland and Abbeyfeale and there was a third ambush at Curranes.

28 Collins's personal notebook, 20 Aug. 1922.

29 *Ibid.*

30 Calton Younger, *Ireland's Civil War*, p. 429.

31 Emmet Dalton interview with author 20/3/1974.

Chapter 4

1 Emmet Dalton interview with author 20/3/1974.

2 Commander-In-Chief wire To Confidence, 21 Aug. 1922, M.P. P7/B/70/52; Mulcahy's response—"these places were under the control of the Royal Engineer Dept...Home Affairs sending a representative by boat today"—M.P. P7/B/70/50. (The response did not arrive until after Collins's death.)

3 Commander-In-Chief wire To Confidence, 21 Aug.

1922, M.P. P7/B/70/37. Mulcahy wanted confirmation when Collins would like this to begin (reconnoitre) and "an understanding that plane will have necessary protection if it lands in Fermoy"—M.P. P7/B/70/34. (Message arrived the day Collins was in West Cork.)

4 Collins's notes—diary, 21 Aug. 1922, now held by Collins's nephew, Michael Collins.

5 *Ibid.*

6 See *Irish Independent*, 16 August, 1922.

7 Dr. D.J. Ahern interview with author 13/6/1974. "Tom was a great friend of mine, we discussed this many times," he said.
See also Cosgrave to Collins, 17 July 1922, M.P. P7/B/29/223; Collins to P. Gov. 16 July 1922, M.P. P7/B/29/224.

8 During the Republican occupation of Cork the *Cork Examiner* was taken over, with Frank Gallagher using space in it for anti-Treaty propaganda. There were appeals to the pro-Treaty forces to join them; each issue bore an editorial note stating that the items appearing under "Republican News" were outside the Editor's control.
From 9 August to 13 August, there was no issue of the *Cork Examiner* printed; when it was in circulation again, the newspaper had a more pro-Treaty stance. *Cork Examiner*: August 8 1922—Issue No.21604; August 9 1922—Issue No. 21605; August 13 1922—Issue No. 21606.

9 Collins's notes—diary, 21 Aug. 1922, now held by Collins's nephew, Michael Collins.

10 Emmet Dalton interview with author 2/4/1974.

11 Collins's notes—diary, 21 Aug. 1922.

12 *Ibid.*

13 Emmet Dalton interview with author 2/4/1974.

14 Desmond Fitzgerald to Commander In Chief, to Acting Chairman, to M. of Finance, 28 July, 1922, M.P. P7a/50.

15 Emmet Dalton interview with author 2/4/1974. When he parted with this information, it was almost in a whisper. Having told the story, he added, "Maybe I shouldn't have told you, as I never told that to anybody."

16 This is Joe Brennan from Bandon, whose signature subsequently graced the Irish £1 notes. See also —Letter from Acting Chairman, Irish Provisional Government, to Collins: "I have reported to Major General Dalton that the following officials have been sent to Cork: Mr. Joseph Brennnan—Ministery of Finance, Treasury; Mr James Lysaght—Local Government, Inspector; Mr T.J. Byrne—Architect, Chief Housing Inspector; Mr M. O' Dwyer —Civil Engineer, (Road, Bridges, etc.); D. Kelly—Medical Inspector; Messrs. Gilligan & Duffy — Petrol; Mr Maurice Jones—Post Office Equipment." 14 Aug. 1922, M.P. P7/B/20/6.

17 Collins's personal notebook, 21 Aug. 1922, now held by Collins's nephew, Michael Collins. See also Collins's note, Monday 21 Aug. 1922. M.P. P7/B/20/6.

18 Emmet Dalton, interview with author 2/4/1974.

19 Collins's notes—diary, 21 August 1922. *The Cork Examiner*, 14 Aug. 1922, reported: "The havoc done at the Cork Telephone Exchange is of a far reaching character. All the lines are unworkable. The fact that there are some miles of poles down must necessarily impede the work." See also Collins's note, Mon. 21 Aug. 1922, M.P. P7a/62.

20 Emmet Dalton interview with author 2/4/1974.

21 Dalton would not disclose details of location or the name

of priest. "We recovered the money, that is sufficient information," he said. Emmet Dalton interview with author 2/4/1974.

Chapter 5

1 Lord Longford and Thomas P. O'Neill, *Eamon de Valera*, p. 198.

2 Domnall MacGiolla Phoill interview with author 23/5/1988.

3 Peter Golden, *Impressions of Ireland*, p 52.

4 *Ibid*, pp 54 to 56.

5 Liam Lynch in letter to his brother Tom, 28 March, 1920. Lynch private family papers.

6 Liam Deasy interview with author 19/9/1973.

7 De Valera wasn't sure if it could be called a meeting as "there were officers meeting all over the country," and he wasn't sure of the "extent of their authority."

8 Paddy O'Sullivan and Donal O'Callaghan were in charge of security outside the house while the meeting was in progress. Interview with author 25/11/1973.

9 Dan Sando O'Donovan interview with author 24/11/1973.

10 Ríobárd Lankford interview with author, 9/12/1973. Ríobárd Lankford, who was attached to the Municipal School, formulated the press, operated the machinery, and had the paper organized weeks before Childers arrived in west Cork. His brother Joe Lankford also helped with the printing press. The secretary was Lena Corcoran.

11 Maggie Sheehan interview with author 28/9/1975.

12 Riobárd Lankford interview with author 9/12/1973.

13 Liam Deasy interview with author 19/9/1973.

14 *Ibid.* Deasy in the course of this interview said that at this time he, like Lynch, harboured the hope that should armaments, which were being organized through American sources, arrive, the scene would be totally changed.

15 Maggie Sheehan interview with author 28/9/1975.

16 Liam Deasy interview with author 19/9/1973.

Chapter 6

1 Collins's notebook, 22 Aug. 1922, held by Collins's nephew, Michael Collins. See also Collins's notes, 22 Aug. 1922, M.P. P7a/62.

2 Emmet Dalton interview with author 2/4/1974.

3 Kate O'Mahony interview with author 26/7/1973. At Ballymichael, Lissarda, Mrs Kate O'Mahony was getting up, she says it was around 8.00 a.m when through the upstairs window she saw the convoy passing.

4 Timmy Kelleher, interview with author 15/4/1974.

5 Known as Denny "The Dane" because there were many families of Longs in the district. His grandfather was a hedge-schoolmaster just beyond Beal na mBláth cross.

6 Timmy Kelleher interview with author 19/4/1974.

7 Newspaper cutting, 23 Aug. 1922, M.P. P7/B/70/27. (Details from John L. O'Sullivan, 31/7/1974). Sean Hales, John L. O'Sullivan, Maurice Collins, Con Slattery and a section of pro-Treaty forces were involved in this operation.

8 Following the plantation, when hundreds of families were moved from England to the fertile lands in the area, the town drew up a charter in 1613. One of its first acts

was to pass a by-law, "That no Roman Catholics be permitted to reside in the town."

9 Timmy Kelleher interview with author 19/4/1974.

Chapter 7

1 Pake Sheehan interview with author 20/4/1974.

2 Liam Deasy interview with author 9/9/1973.

3 Lord Longford & Thomas P. O'Neill, *Eamon de Valera*, p. 199.

4 Bill Powell interview with author, 30/3/1974.

5 *Ibid.*

6 During the War of Independence, one of the tactics of the Flying Columns was: avoid confrontation if unprepared, but if an opportunity arises where an ambush can be successfully laid, then do so; surprise the enemy.

7 Townland: Maulnadrough, commonly known as Bengour East.

8 Jackie Murray interview with author 30/3/1974.

9 Jim Kearney interview with author 11/7/1973.

10 Liam Deasy interview with author, 19/9/1973. Liam Deasy gave this number. Tom Hales in a statement has said, "approximately 40 men formed the ambushing party,"—statement to his brother, Sean Hales—"Report of the Ambush at Beal na Bláth 22nd August 1922; by Tom Hales."

11 Jim Kearney interview with author 11/7/1973 and 31/3/1974. His information corroborated by that of Liam Deasy, 19/9/1973.

12 Siobhán Creedon interview with author 27/3/1979. (After the Civil War Siobhán Creedon married Riobárd Lankford who was responsible for setting up the

Republican printing press. Ríobárd Lankford was in Moneygave on 21st and 22, August when de Valera called before going on to Béal na mBláth.)

13 Siobhán Creedon interview with author 27/3/1979.

14 *Ibid.*

Chapter 8

1 Emmet Dalton interview with author 2/4/1974.

2 *Ibid.* During the War of Independence, Tom Hales and Pat Harte were captured by the Essex Regiment, their nails were pulled off and they were then dragged behind a lorry for some miles. Harte was so badly affected that his mind snapped and he died a few years later.

3 Emmet Dalton, *Freeman's Journal*, 22/8/1923.

4 Emmet Dalton interview with author 2/4/1974.

5 James Cahalane interview with author 19/1/1974.

6 This source is private, as the names of the men consulted by Collins are withheld.

7 See M. Ryan, *The Tom Barry Story*, p. 73.

8 The first Battalion of British Essex Regiment under the command of Major A.E. Percival were drafted into Bandon in January 1920.

9 Michael O'Brien interview with author 8/12/1973.

10 Kathy Hayes interview with author 16/4/1976.

11 Terry Courtney, Charlie O'Shea, Nelius Connolly.

12 Emmet Dalton interview with author 2/4/1974. Collins was about to step into the car when Tim Burke came up to him, and appealed to Collins to try to stop the war which was "tearing families apart."

13 Edith Somerville also had a few words with Jim Wolfe.

Wolfe's parents worked for the Somervilles; Jim was born and reared in a house on the estate. (Somerville & Ross.)

Chapter 9

1 Michael O'Brien interview with author 15/12/1973. (O'Brien, Collins's cousin.).

2 *Ibid.*

3 *Ibid.*

4 *Ibid.*

5 *Ibid.*

6 Jerh. Collins interview with author 16/12/1973.

Chapter 10

1 Jerh. Collins interview with author 16/12/1973.

2 W.T. Cosgrave was acting temporarily as Provisional Government Chairman due to Collins's heavy army duties (decision taken at Provisional Government meeting 12, July1922.) but Collins was to return to active participation and resume his post as both Chairman and Minister of Finance, once the military situation stabilised.

3 Emmet Dalton interview with author 2/4/1974.

4 John L. O'Sullivan interview with author 31/7/1974.

5 *Ibid.*

6 *Ibid.*

7 *Ibid.*

8 Mulcahy to O'Duffy, 31 August 1922, M.P. P7/B/70. The reference to the Lancia is in Dalton to Collins, 14 August 1922, M.P. P7/B/70/58.

9 Con Slattery interview with author 16/1/1975. (Slattery was with Sean Hales's pro-Treaty forces on that day.)

10 John L. O'Sullivan interview with author 31/7/1974.

11 Piarais Beaslai, *Michael Collins and the Making of a New Ireland*, p. 420.

12 Later Fr. T.F. Duggan was appointed Archdeacon of Cork, he went to Peru on the missions in his later years and died 6 months later.

13 Professor Lucy Duggan, interview with author 10/7/1974.

14 Collins to Cosgrave, 5 Aug. 1922, M.P. P7/B/29/87 to P7/B/29/100.

15 Emmet Dalton interview with author 2/4/1974.

16 *Ibid.* On that very day the *Independent* reported: "Rumours concerning peace overtures are still afloat, but they are discountenanced in trustworthy quarters. Citizens generally feel that the hour of compromise has long since struck, and that there can be no peace until the military operations are successfully and completely ended. It is indeed idle talk of peace when the wholesale destruction of property continues daily ..."

17 Emmet Dalton interview with author 2/4/1974.

18 Jim Wolfe interview with author 29/3/1974.

19 The author interviewed the following men who participated in the ambush: Jim Kearney, 12/5/1973, 11/7/1973, 24/2/1974, 10/3/1974, 31/3/1974, 19/4/1974, 12/5/1974, 7/6/1974, 14/6/1974, 27/6/1974, 10/7/1974, 14/9/1974, 1/12/1974, 28/12/1974, 31/3/1975, 2/7/1975, 9/3/1975, 2/7/1975, 13/2/1976.
Timmy Sullivan, 18/8/1973, 16/2/1974, 31/2/1974, 11/3/1974, 29/3/1974, 20/4/1974, 12/5/1974, 13/6/1974, 18/1/1975.
Tom Kelleher, 11/11/1973, 16/2/1974, 17/3/1974, 19/4/

1974, 6/6/1974.

Liam Deasy, 5/12/1973, 9/1/1974, 7/2/1974.

Jim Wolfe, 9/3/1974, 29/3/1974, 22/4/1974, 19/5/1974, 20/7/1974, 22/9/1974.

Bill Powell, 8/12/1973, 10/7/1974, 14/9/1974, 15/3/1975, 2/5/1976.

Charlie Foley, 16/11/1974, 7/6/1975, 4/10/1975, 23/5/1976.

Tom Foley, *Ibid.*

Emmet Dalton, 2/4/1974, 4/4/1974, 20/4/1974.

Pat Buttimer, 17/3/1974, 6/6/1974.

Sean Hyde, 13/7/1974, 20/7/1974.

Jim Carmody, 21/7/1974.

Con Murphy 4/9/1974.

Dan O'Callaghan, 25/4/1975.

Con Michael Murphy, 13/9/1974.

Jack Murray, 27/7/1974, 29/11/1974, 9/7/1975.

Tom Murray, 29/11/1974, 19/7/1975.

Patrick Mahony, 9/7/1975.

Patk. Desmond 9/7/1975.

Reps. John McPeake, 21/5/1976.

Jim Hurley, Statement and notes, 1948.

Freeman's Journal 22 August, 1923.

20 Commandant Peter Young, letter to author 10 March 1988—details from Military archives.

21 Sean O'Connell, RTE. archives.

Chapter 11

1 Emmet Dalton interview with author 4/4/1974.

2 Tom Kelleher interview with author 20/10/1973.

3 Liam Deasy interview with author 19/9/1973.

4 Jim Kearney interview with author 11/9/1973 and 24/2/1974.

5 Sean O'Connell, RTE archives.

6 Emmet Dalton, *Freeman's Journal*, 22/8/1923.

7 Emmet Dalton interview with author 4/4/1974.

8 Bill Powell interview with author 30/11/1973.

9 *Ibid.*

10 *Ibid.*

11 Other writings have mentioned Crookstown instead of Cloughduv. This may have been because the convoy intended to travel through Crookstown in the morning, and in the night-time confusion they were unaware of their location.

12 Bill Powell interview with author 30/3/1974.

13 Jim Carmody interview with author 10/6/1974.

14 *Ibid.*

15 Emmet Dalton document written by him, his own private collection—viewed 4/4/1974.

16 Emmet Dalton interview with author 4/4/1974.

17 *Ibid.* Over the years questions have been asked as to whether the last rites of the Catholic Church had been administered to the late Michael Collins. Dalton said he did not discuss this event over the years; the abortive event at Cloughduv over-shadowed, for him, this moment at Victoria Cross. (He says he decided "not to give interviews" over the years.)

18 D.V. Horgan interview with author 21/4/1982.

19 Dr. Leo Ahern had been a house-surgeon in the Mercy hospital. When the troops landed in Cork Dr. Leo Ahern commandeered Shanakiel Hospital on behalf of the Provisional Government. He went to Dr. Dunden, under whom he worked in the Mercy Hospital and made arrangements that the seriously injured pro-Treaty army men would be treated at the Mercy Hospital, and Shanakiel would be a type of convalescing home for

minor injuries, "what the army would call, a casualty clearing station."

20 Jim Wolfe interview with author 9/3/1974.

21 Emmet Dalton interview with author 4/4/1974. At Portobello Barracks when Richard Mulcahy, Chief of Staff, received the news of Michael Collins's death at 1.15 a.m. (23 August), he wrote a notice for the army and the people:

Stand Calmly by Your Posts. Bend bravely and undaunted to your work. Let no cruel act of reprisal blemish your bright honour. Every dark hour that Michael Collins met since 1916 seemed to steel that bright strength of his and temper his gay bravery. You are left each inheritors of that strength, and of that bravery. To each of you falls his unfinished work. No darkness in the hour—no loss of comrades will daunt you at it, Ireland! The Army serves—strengthened by its sorrow.

22 Emmet Dalton interview with author 4/4/1974.

23 *Ibid.*

Chapter 12

1 Mrs Duggan, interview with author 27/7/1975. Mrs Duggan, Warrenscourt, and her husband Con Duggan were owners of Shanakiel Hospital. They still have the crucifix in their home.

2 Dr. Leo Ahern interview with author 18/5/1976. Dr. Leo Ahern said they had "a difficult journey" to Dublin as they had to make several detours due to road obstructions.

3 Fr. Joe Ahern interview with author 4/9/1976. Later Fr. Joe Ahern was appointed Canon in Aherla.

4 Dr. Gerard Ahern interview with author 24/4/1976. (Brother of Dr. Leo Ahern.)

5   Letter from Hazel P. Smyth to author 15/1/1975. "The reason it was brought from Cork by boat was that the railways were disrupted at the time owing to the political situation ... *The Classic* was employed only intermittently on the Liverpool/Cork run from June 1921 to 1924, when it remained in the company for seven years."

6   Dalton wire to General Staff 9 a.m. on 23/8/1922. M.P. P7/B/70/39.

7   Later Fr. Joseph Scannell was appointed Dean of Cork.

8   Ernest Blythe interview with author 9/1/1974.

9   Oliver St. John Gogarty, *As I was going down Sackville Street*, p. 183.

10 Ulick O'Connor, *Oliver St. John Gogarty*, p 205. According to Ulick O'Connor, during the early part of 1922, "Gogarty and Collins would drive out for tea" on evenings to W.T. Cosgrave's house at Beechpark. Here for a short period they would forget the problems of public life, and according to Cosgrave, "Collins would roar with laughter at Gogarty's sallies, particularly when Gogarty said something more than usually irreverent that caused a shadow to flit across the face of the Vice-President"—p.202.

11 Ernest Blythe interview with author 9/1/1974.

12 Oliver St. John Gogarty, *As I was going down Sackville Street*, p.183.

13 Ernest Blythe interview with author 9/1/1974.

14 Sir John Lavery, *The Life of a Painter*, pp. 216, 217.

15 Elizabeth, Countess of Fingall, *Seventy Years Young*, p. 408.

16 *Ibid.* p. 409.

17 Sir John Lavery, *The Life of a Painter*, p. 217.

18 *Ibid.*

19 Emmet Dalton interview with author 20/4/1974.

20 Daily newspapers. See also M. P. p7a/64. (Canon Sean Piggott remembers the large numbers of priests in black —not in soutanes. He said many Irish priests returned home from around the world to the funeral.)

21 Griffith's death only preceded Collins's by ten days.

Chapter 13

1 The author interviewed the following for details of what happened directly after the ambush: Jim Kearney, op. cit.; Timmy Sullivan, op. cit.; Bill Powell, op. cit.; Charlie Foley, op. cit.; Tom Foley, op. cit.; Liam Deasy, op. cit.; Tom Kelleher, op. cit.; Sean Hyde, op. cit.; Pake Sheehan, op. cit.; Jim Doyle, 7/12/1974; Tom Barry, op. cit.; Con Murphy, op. cit.; Michael Murphy, op. cit.; Mary O'Neill Walsh, 16/6/1974; Ned Galvin, 15/2/1974; Tom Taylor, 2/7/1975; Denis Lordan 7/7/1974; Jackie Murray, op. cit.; Tom Murray, op. cit.

2 Bill Powell interview with author 14/9/1974.

3 Liam Deasy interview with author 19/9/1973.

4 *Ibid.*

Chapter 14

1 Liam Lynch's original letter to Liam Deasy 28 August 1922, Military Archives, Cathal Brugha Barracks, Lot 4/3. Liam Lynch to Liam Deasy, Deasy private papers, 28 August 1922. See also M.P. P7a/81, and Eoin Neeson, *The Sunday Review*, 11 January 1959.

2 *Ibid.*

3 *Ibid.*

4 Collins memo, 10 Aug. 1922, M.P. P7/B/2.

5 Frank Aiken to Richard Mulcahy, 27 Aug. 1922, M.P. P7a/178. Frank Aiken appealed to Mulcahy "to stop the struggle" and said he would "die in order to prove" his own sincerity and that of "the men opposed to you."

6 Piaras Beaslai, *Michael Collins*, p. 436.

7 Jim Kearney interview with author 19/4/1974.

8 Timmy Sullivan interview with author 22/6/1974.

9 Emmet Dalton interview with author 20/4/1974.

10 Some time after Collins's death a wooden cross was stuck into the soil beside the spot where he fell. Later a local committee painted a cement stone with a black cross on it. This stone was erected at a part of the road which was reasonably wide, but at the opposite side of the road from where Collins fell, and quite a distance north. It was beside this stone that the present monument was erected. Here an annual commemoration ceremony is held as near as possible to 22 August.

11 Collins to O'Duffy, 17 Aug. 1922, M.P. P7/B/21/8.

12 Collins has a note in his diary, "To speak Capt. C.—unprepared escort." Wednesday, 23, August, 1922. Obviously he intended taking the matter up with Captain Coghlan on his return to Portobello Barracks, M.P. P7a/62.

13 Emmet Dalton interview with author 20/4/1974.

14 Ernest Blythe interview with author 20/3/1974.

15 Jim Wolfe interview with author 9/3/1974.

16 Dr. Leo Ahern interview with author 20/5/1976. (I spent a considerable amount of time questioning Dr. Leo Ahern at his London flat.)

17 Dr. Michael Riordan details 7/3/1974.

18 Dr. Christy Kelly interview with author 14/1/1974.

19 Dr. Gerard Ahern interview with author 29/4/1976.

20 A representative of the late Dr. Cagney, 16/1/1976 (name withheld by request.)

21 Margery Forester, *Michael Collins: The Lost Leader*, p 343.

22 Dr. Leo Ahern interview with author 20/5/1976. Dr. Leo Ahern says he has no recollection of any discussion with Dr. Gogarty who "had to get on with his task," while he (Dr. Leo) had to attend to other "pressing business in connection with the funeral."

23 Ulick O'Connor, *Oliver St. John Gogarty*, p. 206.

24 Dr. Gerard Ahern interview with author 2/5/1976.

25 Emmet Dalton, interview with Cathal O'Shannon, RTE documentary.

26 Ray Smith & Jim Nicholl, *The Irish Independent*, 20 May, 1971.

27 Oliver Snoddy letter to the author 9/4/1974

28 Oliver Snoddy letter to the author 21/5/1974

29 Brother Allen interview with author 3/4/1976.

30 Edward C. Smith was an agent for a business firm in Cork, and was a past pupil of O'Connell School, Dublin, and close friend of Brother Allen.

31 Each house in a parish took and still takes a turn to have "The Stations."

32 Oliver Snoddy letter to the author 9/4/1974

33 The author has a statement made by Tom Hales to his brother Major General Sean Hales: " ... The Column had pulled out of position and only a few men of a rearguard

party were there when the car came in sight. They knew they had killed an officer of very high rank with one of the last shots fired but they had no idea who that officer was." Dated 22 August 1922.

34 Liam Deasy interview with author 19/9/1973. "We regretted the type of bullet used. These were picked up after ambushes during the Tan War," he said. Deasy said that Sonny Neill personally described the event to the IRA's Chief Intelligence Officer, Sean Dowling, when he journeyed to West Cork in September 1922. This information was confirmed by Seamus O'Donovan, G.H.Q.—interview with author 5/6/1975.

35 Tom Barry interview with author 17/4/1976. Following his escape from Maryboro prison in Sept. 1922, Barry got full details of Collins's death. He told me, "Sonny Neill got Collins." The following also gave this information to the author: Jim Kearney, 31/3/1974; Timmy Sullivan, 12/5/1974; Tom Kelleher, 6/6/1974; Bill Powell, 15/3/1975; Jackie Murray, 29/11/1974; Denis Lordan, 7/7/1974; Sean Hyde 13/7/1974; Con Murphy 9/9/1974; Pat Buttimer, 6/6/1974; Dan Cahalane, 17/9/1977, Tom Murray 29/3/1975; Jim Doyle 18/4/1976.

Postscript

1. Tom Barry interview with author 10/4/1976.

2. Emmet Dalton interview with author 20/3/1974.

3. *Ibid.*

4. Liam Lynch letter to his brother Tom, 27 October 1922. Lynch private family papers.

5. Free State Order, 7 October 1922: "If prisoners are taken they must not be released until they are incapable of further harm. If executions are necessary they must be carried out with no fear of the chimera of popular reaction."

6. Lord Longford and Thomas P. O'Neill, *Eamon de Valera*, p. 201.

7. Liam Lynch letter to his brother Tom, 28 October 1922.

8. Ernest Blythe interview with author 20/30/1974.

9. General Order, 30 November 1923. P7a/83, M.P. (Lynch wrote to the Provisional Government on 27 November: "As your Parliament and Army Headquarters well know, we on our side have at all times adhered to the recognised rules of warfare. In the early days of this war we took hundreds of your forces prisoners but accorded them all the right of prisoners of war and, over and above, treated them as fellow countrymen and former comrades ... But the prisoners you have taken have been treated barbarously, and when helpless you have tortured, wounded and murdered them ...")

10. Richard Mulcahy signed the following order, 7 December, 1923: "You are hereby notified that being a person taken in arms against the Government, you will be executed at 8 am on Friday, 8 December as a reprisal for the assassination of Brigadier Sean Hales T.D. in Dublin, on 7 December on his way to a meeting of Dáil Eireann and as a solemn warning to those associated with you and who are engaged in a conspiracy of assassination against the representatives of the Irish people.

    — Richard Mulcahy, General Chief of Staff."

Bibliography

Primary Sources

Manuscript Sources University College, Dublin, Archives
Ernest Blythe Papers
Richard Mulcahy Papers
Miscellaneous material

Trinity College, Dublin, Records Office
Erskine Childers Papers

National Library of Ireland
Michael Collins Papers
Joseph McGarrity Papers
Kathleen MacKenna Napoli Papers

Public Records
Records of the Ministry and Cabinet of Dáil Eireann in the
   State Paper Office, Dublin
Colonial Office Papers, Public Record Office, London
British Library Board Newspaper Library

Private Manuscripts
General Michael Collins, Note Books, held by Michael
   Collins, nephew of General Michael Collins
Liam Lynch Papers
Jim Kearney Papers (Letters)
Dr. Gerard Ahern Papers

Diarmuid Brennan Papers & Letters

Dr. Ned Barret Papers

Bill Hales Papers

Sean Hales Notes

D.V. Horgan Papers

Jim Hurley Statement & Notes

Military Archives Material received from Commandant Peter Young, Cathal Brugha Barracks, Dublin.

RTE Archives

Newspapers & Periodicals
The Irish Times; The Irish Independent; The Freeman's Journal; The Cork Examiner; The Sunday Express; The Daily Sketch; The Daily Mail; The Sunday Review; The Sunday Independent; The Sunday Press; The Clare Champion; The Limerick Leader; The Southern Star; The Capuchin Annual.

Oral Testimony
My reliance has been on the many people who gave unselfishly of their time, some of whom allowed themselves to be quizzed rather vigorously on their observations of events at, and surrounding the Beal na mBláth ambush; their contribution has been essential. Their names are cited in the Acknowledgements and Notes.

Secondary Sources

Andrews, C.S. *Dublin Made Me*. Cork & Dublin: The Mercier Press,1979

Barry, Tom. *Guerilla Days In Ireland.*, Dublin: *Irish Press*,1949.

Barry, Tom. *The Reality of the Anglo-Irish War, 1920-21, in West Cork: Refutations, Corrections and Comment on*

Liam Deasy's ' "Towards Ireland Free." Tralee 1974.

Beaslai, Piaras. *Michael Collins and the Making of a New Ireland.*, Dublin: The Phoenix Publishing Co. 1926.

Bell, J. Bowyer. *The Secret Army.* Dublin: Poolbeg, 1989.

Bennet, George. *The History of Bandon.* Cork: Frances Guy, 1869.

Bennett, Richard. *The Black and Tans.* London: New English Library, 1970.

Boyce, D.G. *Nationalism in Ireland.* London, 1982.

Bowman, John. *De Valera and the Ulster Question.* 1917-73. Oxford: Oxford University Press, 1982.

Breen, Dan. *My Fight For Irish Freedom.* Tralee: Anvil Books Ltd, 1964, 1982.

Brennan, Michael. *The War in Clare 1911—1921.* Dublin 1980.

Butler, Ewan. *Barry's Flying Column..* London: Burns & Oates, 1961.

Brinton, Crane. *The Anatomy of Revolution.* London 1953.

Collins, Michael. *The Path To Freedom.* Cork & Dublin: The Mercier Press, 1968

Coogan, Tim Pat. *Ireland Since the Rising.* London: Pall Mall, 1966.

Coogan, Tim Pat. *The I.R.A.* London: Fontana, 1971.

Cronin, Seán, *The McGarrity Papers*, Tralee: Anvil Books, 1972.

Crozier, Brigadier General F.P. *Ireland Forever.* London: Cape, 1932.

Curran, J. M. *The Birth of the Irish Free State.* 1921-1923, U.S.A.: Alabama 1980.

Deasy, Liam. *Towards Ireland Free.* Cork & Dublin: The Mercier Press, 1979.

Deasy, Liam. *Brother Against Brother.* Cork & Dublin: The Mercier Press, 1982.

Dwyer, T. Ryle. *Eamon de Valera*. Dublin: Gill & Macmillan, 1980.

Dwyer, T. Ryle. *Michael Collins and The Treaty: His Difference with De Valera*. Cork & Dublin: The Mercier Press, 1981.

Farrell, Michael. *Northern Ireland*, The Orange State. London 1975.

Feehan, John M. *The Shooting of Michael Collins—Murder or Accident?* Dublin & Cork: The Mercier Press, 1981.

Fingall, Elizabeth, Countess. *Seventy Years Young*. London: Collins, 1937.

Forester, Margery. *Michael Collins: The Lost Leader*. London: Sidgwick & Jackson, 1971.

Gaughan, J.A. *Austin Stack: Portrait of a Separatist*. : Dublin 1977.

Gogarty, Oliver St. John. *As I was going down Sackville Street*. London: Rich & Cowen, 1937.

Greaves, C.D. *Liam Mellows and the Irish Revolution*, London: Lawrence & Wishart, 1971.

Hopkinson, Michael. *Green Against Green*. Dublin: Gill & Macmillan, 1988.

Kee, Robert. *Ourselves Alone; The Green Flag*. vol. 3. London: Quartet Books, 1976.

Lavery, Sir John. *The Life of a Painter*, London: Cassell, 1940.

Lawlor, Sheila. *Britain and Ireland*, 1914-23, Dublin: Gill & Macmillan, 1983.

Longford, Earl of, and O'Neill, Thomas P. *Eamon de Valera*. Dublin: Gill & Macmillan, 1970.

Morrison, George. *The Irish Civil War: An Illustrated History*, Dublin: 1981.

Lyons, F.S. *Ireland Since the Famine*. London: Collins/Fontana, 1973.

Macardle, Dorothy. *The Irish Republic*. London: Corgi, 1968.

MacEoin, Uinseann, Ed. *Survivors*. Dublin: Argenta Publications, 1980.

Macready, General Sir Nevil. *Annals of an Active Life*. London: Hutchinson, 1942.

Murphy, John A. *Ireland in the Twentieth Century*. Dublin: Gill & Macmillan, 1975.

Neeson, Eoin. *The Civil War 1922-1923*. Dublin: Poolbeg, 1989.

Neeson, Eoin. *The Life & Death of Michael Collins*. Cork & Dublin: The Mercier Press, 1968.

Neligan, Dave. *The Spy in the Castle*. London: MacGibbon & Kee, 1968.

O'Broin, Leon. *Michael Collins*. Dublin: Gill & Macmillan, 1980.

O'Broin, Leon, Ed. *In Great Haste: The Letters of Michael Collins and Kitty Kiernan*. Dublin: Gill & Macmillan, 1983.

O'Connor, Batt. *With Michael Collins in the Fight for Irish Independence*. London: Peter Davis, 1929.

O'Connor, Ulick. *A Terrible Beauty is Born*. London: Hamish Hamilton, 1975.

O'Connor, Ulick. *Oliver St. John Gogarty*. London: Granada, 1981.

O'Donoghue, Florence. *No Other Law*. Dublin: The Irish Press Ltd., 1956.

O' Halloran, Clare. *Partition and the Limits of Irish Nationalism*. Dublin: Gill & Macmillan, 1987.

O'Hegarty, P.S. *The Victory of Sinn Fein*. Dublin: Talbot Press, 1924.

O'Malley, Ernie. *On Another Man's Wound*. Tralee: Anvil Books, 1972.

O'Malley, Ernie. *The Singing Flame*. Tralee: Anvil Books, 1979.

Pakenham, Frank *Peace by Ordeal*. London: Sidgwick & Jackson, 1972.

Ryan, Desmond. *Sean Treacy and the Third Tipperary Brigade, I.R.A.* Tralee 1945.

Ryan, Meda. *The Tom Barry Story.* Cork & Dublin: The Mercier Press, 1982.

Ryan, Meda. *The Real Chief—The Story of Liam Lynch.* Cork & Dublin: The Mercier Press, 1986.

Shakespeare, Sir Geoffery. *Let Candles Be Brought In.* London: MacDonald, 1949.

Talbot, Hayden. *Michael Collins' Own Story.* London: Hutchinson, 1923.

Taylor, Rex. *Michael Collins—The Big Fellow.* London: Four Square, 1961.

Taylor, Rex. *Assassination.* London:1961.

Younger, Calton. *Ireland's Civil War.* London: Muller Ltd, 1972.

INDEX

Cosgrave, W.T., 24-5, 27, 37, 123
  Collins to, 19, 55, 57-8, 92-3
  Chairman Provisional Government, 23, 148
  and Collins's cap, 141, 144
  President of Dail, 147, 148
Craig, Gardner & Co. 5
Creedon, Michael, 77
Creedon, Siobhan, 77
Crofts, Tom, 76, 128, 155
Crosbie, Tom, 55
Crowley, Dinny, 72
Crowley, John 1
Cullen, Tom, 18
Cumann na mBan, 5, 76, 83, 151
Cumann na nGaedhael, 150
Customs and Excise funds, 55, 56

Dail Eireann, 8, 73, 147
  Treaty debate, 14
  postponement proposed, 92-3
Dalton, Charlie, 111
Dalton, Emmet, 12, 25, 123, 133, 136, 146-7, 151
  and Wilson assassination, 20
  active in Cork, 27-8, 36, 40
  at Béal na mBláth, 32, 96, 101-2, 105, 132
  Collins visit, 51-3, 54
  on inspection tour, 55-6, 65-6, 70, 81, 85, 91, 93
  on Collins, 58, 79-80, 83, 93, 98-90
  death of Collins, 106-13, 116
  informs of Collins's death, 114-15, 118
  on Collins's death, 118-19, 140-41
  cap of, 141-2

Dalton, Frank, 58
Daly, Liam, 69-70, 144
Davis, Crompton Llewylen, 3
Davis, Moira O'Connor, 3
de Valera, Eamon, 9, 10, 14, 128
  and treaty, 11
  Collins pact, 16
  in Cork, 60, 61, 62,-4, 77
  on Collins, 60, 62, 76-8
  meets Deasy, 63-4
  at Béal na mBláth, 72-4
  working for peace, 147
  Republican President, 148
  surrender, 149-50
de Valera, Sinead, 9
Deasy, Liam, 10, 16, 22, 49, 62, 160
  and de Valera, 61, 63-4
  plans Collins' ambush, 72-8
  at Béal na mBláth, 76-7, 95, 102-3, 106, 108-9, 132
  Collins on, 92
  after Béal na mBlath, 126-7, 128, 130
  on Collins's death, 145
  surrender, 149
Dempsey, Pat, 153
Doherty, Bobs, 103
Dolan, Joe, 17, 46, 53, 65, 123
  at Béal na mBláth, 102-3, 107
Donoghue, Mike, 103
Donoghue, Sean, 151
Dowling, 114
Dublin Castle, 7, 8
Duggan, Fr. T.F., 92
Duggan, Prof. Lucy, 92
Dunne, Reginald, 17-20, 37-8

Easter Rising, 1916, 5-6
Ennis, Tom, 136, 146, 151

THE CIVIL WAR 1922-23

Eoin Neeson

Using material scrupulously culled from contemporary sources (newspaper, archival, eye-witness accounts, interviews, field dispatches), Eoin Neeson's now-classic narrative history of Ireland's Civil War appears revised and updated since its first publication in 1966.

Step by tragic step, we witness the unfolding drama and birthpangs of Ireland's nationhood: the Truce ending the War of Independence and the Treaty negotiotions of 1921; the Dáil debates and widening split between Republicans (anti-Treatyites) and Free Staters (pro-Treatyites); the fall of the Four Courts, opening salvoes, and alignments of Church, Press, Industry and Army; the summer campaign in the field as the war front moves south from Dublin to Wicklow, Wexford, Waterford and Tipperary, to the fastnesses of Cork, Kerry and the 'Munster Republic'; the tragic death of Michael Collins, the descent into guerrilla skirmishing, executions and their legacy — all are skilfully documented and assessed.

No understanding of Ireland's contemporary history and politics is possible without a knowledge of the crucial events of the Civil War years. The detail and clarity of Eoin Neeson's masterly appraisal make Civil War 1922-23 a compelling and riveting read.

POOLBEG

THE SECRET ARMY

J. Bowyer Bell

The Secret Army is the definitive work on the IRA. It provides an absorbing account of a movement which has had a profound effect on the shaping of the modern Irish state. J. Bowyer Bell, a specialist in the problems of unconventional war, terrorism, risk analysis and crisis management, has been a research scholar at Harvard and MIT and at the Institute of War and Peace Studies, Columbia University. He is now President of the International Analysis Centre in New York. He has written more than a dozen books, including *Assassin! The Theory and Practice of Political Violence* and *The Gun in Politics: An Analysis of Irish Political Conflict 1916-1986.*

POOLBEG